To our parents, families (including dogs), and friends -
Thanks for making life so wonderful!

Published by

Perpetual Motion
PO Box 600
Hailey, ID 83333
mcbob@sunvalley.net

ISBN# 0-9665953-1-9
$10.95 U.S. Dollars
$737.92 Nepalese Rupees
$1689.15 Spanish Pesetas

Cover design by Darla McRoberts
Book layout, design and authored by Greg & Darla McRoberts
Maps by Greg McRoberts
Edited by Dude, Dude, Meg and Fupper

Table of contents

The Winter Guide

The Elephants Perch, Sawtooth Mountains - The McBob Collection

Important Phone Numbers

Emergencies... 911
Avalanche Report... (208) 788-1200 x.8027
Web: http://www.avalanche.org
Sawtooth National Recreation Area .... (208) 727-5000
Stanley Ranger District................................ (208) 774-3681
Local Winter Road Report .... (208) 886-2266
Idaho State Road Report................................ (208) 336-6600
National Weather Service - Boise Forcast... (208) 342-8303
Ketchum Ranger District............................... (208) 622-5371
Lost River Ranger District .... (208) 588-2224
Yankee Fork Ranger District......................... (208) 838-2201
Blaine County Sheriff.................................... (208) 788-5555
Wood River Medical Center........................... (208) 788-2222
　　　　or　　　　　　　　　　　　　　(208) 622-3333
Ketchum Area Chamber of Commerce........ (208) 726-3423
　　　　or　　　　　　　　　　　　　　(800) 634-3347
Hailey Chamber of Commerce...................... (208) 788-2700
Bellevue Chamber of Commerce.................. (208) 788-7060
Stanley Sawtooth Chamber of Commerce... (208) 774-3411

How To Use This Guidebook

This guidebook was designed, hopefully, with ease-of-use in mind. If you could gather from the Table of Contents, located before this page, you will notice the layout of the book:

- An overview map to orient you in the Sun Valley area.
- A historical perspective to help you appreciate what you see in the area.
- **General Information:** Hotels, Restaurants, etc.
- **Summer Guide:** Activities listed alphabetically.
- **Winter Guide:** Activities listed alphabetically.

**Please keep in mind that when we talk about the Wood River Valley, we are referring to the entire geographical area: Bellevue, Hailey, Ketchum and Sun Valley. Just remember Sun Valley is 1.5 miles from Ketchum, just 13.5 miles from Hailey and 16.5 miles from Bellevue.

Hopefully this will help you find the information you want quick and easily.
Enjoy!

Introduction and Acknowledgments

From the title of this section, it seems there is quite a bit to pack into such a small area. But in reality, this is a guidebook and not a novel so we won't be taking up too much of your precious time. Let's get to the point:

This guidebook was written in response to the wants of many readers of our Sun Valley area mountain bike guidebook, *Good Dirt*. It seems that there has been a demand for a comprehensive guide for the Sun Valley area which covers all aspects of a typical visit. From a dining and hotel reference area, to backcountry skiing and rock climbing, the information contained in this book will help you plan and organize your trip to the area all the way to the babysitter.

We have made every effort to make this guidebook as accurate as humanly possible, but please keep in mind that resort towns are known for high business turnover. A business that was thriving at the time of this writing may be gone in a year. However, in the event we did miss something or had some inaccurate information, please pass it along to us for the next printing, as all information is helpful. You can send us the information through the postal service or email. All pertinent information is located on the second page of this guidebook.

We would like to thank all the local business owners, community volunteers and people of the Wood River and Sawtooth Valleys for their help and support in writing this guidebook. This book is for you.

Stanley Lake - The McBob Collection

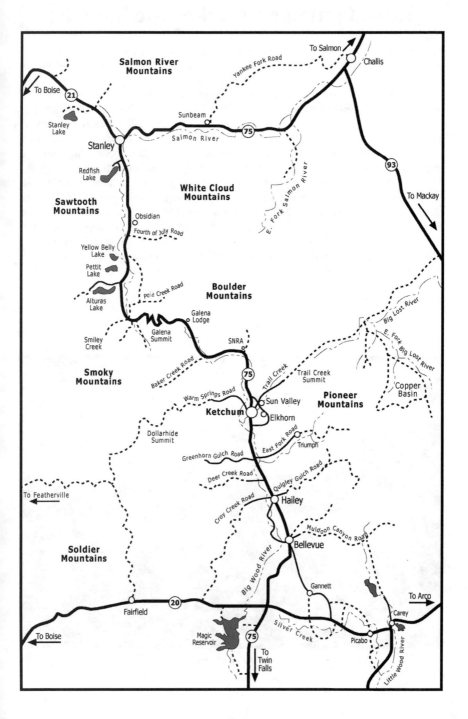

8

Sun Spots

The Adventurous Travelers Guide to Sun Valley, Idaho

Getting To / From Sun Valley

Sun Valley is located in the central Idaho mountains, just north of the Snake River plain. There are four towns which make up the Wood River Valley: Bellevue, Hailey, Ketchum and Sun Valley. Ketchum is the main destination town for travelers, with the resort/hotel area of Sun Valley located one mile from downtown Ketchum.

By Air

Friedman Memorial Airport is located in Hailey, approximately 12 miles south of Ketchum. Currently, only two commercial airlines fly into the Wood River Valley: Skywest, and Horizon Air.

Skywest has connecting flights into Hailey via Salt Lake City, one of the main hubs for Delta Airlines. There are numerous flights daily during the week and increased flights on weekends and holidays. Horizon Air offers daily flight service into Hailey through Boise, as well as a weekend direct flight service from Seattle. Rates and schedules can and do change, so your best bet is to call ahead. On holidays the flights can get extremely full and trying to fly stand-by is very difficult. In other words, plan ahead and stick to your schedule.

Winter weather is another major factor when flying into Friedman Memorial Airport. Intense snowstorms can keep the airport closed for days, at which point flights are diverted to either Twin Falls or Boise. Passengers must then ride a charter bus to the Hailey airport provided by the airlines.

By Land

Most travelers to the Wood River Valley arrive by car. The most popular route is via Interstate 84 from either Salt Lake City or Boise. If you are coming in from Salt Lake City, drive to Twin Falls and turn north on Highway 75. Follow this road directly into the Wood River Valley. If road conditions are good, then it should take you about 5+ hours from Salt Lake City.

If you are coming from Boise, you have two obvious choices. Drive east to Twin Falls on I-84 until you see the turnoff for Highway 75 north. This highway will take you on a journey through fields and desert to the Wood River Valley. The other choice is a bit more exciting and in the winter can be rather treacherous, however, it is the more popular route to Sun Valley. Take I-84 from Boise to Mountain Home and turn off onto Highway 20 and follow it to the intersection with Highway 75 (blinking light). Turn left and cruise into the valley.

In winter when roads are bad, take the Twin Falls route to avoid the use of a tow truck or wrecker from the Highway 20 route due to drifting snow. However, if you're not in a hurry and enjoy beautiful scenery, another option is available.

During the fair-weather months only (not winter), travelers can drive from Boise to Idaho City, and then to Stanley. When you intersect Highway 75 in Stanley, turn right and head south. It is about 60 miles up and over Galena Summit into Ketchum It takes about 3 1/2 hours from Boise to Sun Valley. This road gets heavily avalanched during the winter months and remains closed most of the time.

Airlines Information

Access Air: (Web: access-air.com)........................... (800) 307-4984
Air Ketchum: (Web: airketchum.com)................... (888) 701-2494
Horizon Air: (Web: alaska-air.com)
    Passenger Information & Reservations....... (800) 547-9308
    Flight Information Line (local).................... (208) 788-1352
    Baggage Service Line................................. (208) 788-2051
Northwest Airlines: (Web: nwa.com)...................... (800) 225-2525
Skywest Airlines: (Web: skywest.com)
    Passenger Information & Reservations....... (800) 453-9417
    Flight Status Hotline (local)........................ (208) 788-4887
    Package Pick-up & Delivery........................ (800) 638-7346
Southwest Airlines: (Web: iflyswa.com)................. (800) 435-9792
United Airlines: (Web: ual.com)............................. (800) 241-6522
Friedman Memorial Airport................................... (208) 788-4956
Magic Valley Regional Airport (Twin Falls)......... (208) 733-5215

Airport Transportation / Taxi / Rental Car Information

A-1 Taxi.. (208) 726-9351
Bald Mountain Taxi & Limo................................. (208) 726-2650
Sun Valley Express (Boise Shuttle Service)........... (208) 622-VANS
            or   (877) 622-VANS
email:vans@sunvalleyexpress.com, web: sunvalex.com
Sun Valley Stages...................................... (800) 574-8661
Sun Valley Hosts....................................... (208) 726-4444
email: host@sunvalley.net, web: sunvalleyhost.com
Wild Country Shuttle................................ (208) 720-1566
Avis Rent A Car .... (800) 831-2847
    at Friedman Memorial Airport (208) 788-2382
Budget... (800) 527-0700
    at Friedman Memorial Airport (208) 788-3660
Hertz.. (800) 654-3131
    at Friedman Memorial Airport (208) 788-4548
Practical Rent-A-Car................................ (800) 437-7136
    at Friedman Memorial Airport (208) 788-3224
Thrifty... (800) 634-6539

Local Bus Service

KART (Ketchum Area Rapid Transit) is the local bus service providing free transportation around the Ketchum area. All buses are ski-equiped and have stopping points all over the place. Schedules vary by location but run about every 15-minutes in town and every 30-minutes the further out you get. Pick up a schedule at one of the many locations around town, or at the Ketchum Chamber of Commerce at the corner of 4th & Main St.

Weather - When Best to Visit?

Sun Valley is a mountainous resort town, which means the weather can change at the blink of an eye. We have the typical cold winters and mild summers you will find in any mountain town, including mud and leaf season. Here is some seasonal weather information to help you plan your trip accordingly:

January - Cold and snowy, usually the best powder days for skiing.

February - Cold and snowy, with occasional warm days. Still great skiing.

March - Warmer, wet-snow days. Transition weather time where Mother Nature can't make up her mind whether it should snow, sleet, rain, or be gorgeous.

April - Warmer, mild days, highs in the 50-60's. Skiing in t-shirts and crust-cruising in the backcountry. Late April signals the beginning of mud-season, slack hours at businesses and locals splitting town for a month to go south to the Mexican warmth.

May - Warmer days, highs in the 60-70's and serious mud-season. North valley trails aren't clear of snow yet, but south valley trails are open for biking, etc.

June - Warm days, highs in the 70's, and north area trails begin to clear. This is dependent on the type of winter we've had. Businesses are in full-bloom, locals are back and wildflowers are showing their colors. A gorgeous time of year.

July - The height of summertime in Sun Valley. Highs are in the 80's, the town gets booming, the trails are all open and there are tons of things to do.

August - Summer is in full swing with highs in the 80's to low 90's. The area is still booming with people but crowds slowly start to thin out around the end of the month. The backcountry trails are still amazing.

September - Fall is in the air now and highs are in the 70's with the lows at night dipping into the 40's and 50's. Leaves are starting to change and town is definitely slowing down. A great time for deals at the stores.

October - Fall is here with highs in the 50's and low's hitting mid 30's. Slack has begun again with locals and businesses. Some restaurants and shops close down for a few weeks. Snow starts falling in the high mountains.

November - Early winter has begun with highs in the 40's and night temperatures reaching the low 30's. Businesses are opening back up around the middle of the month, with town booming again by Thanksgiving. The skiing starts on Thanksgiving Day on Bald Mountain, and sometimes the backcountry is skiable at this point.

December - Winter is here and so are the crowds for the holiday season. As Christmas gets nearer, parking can be a problem. Temperatures can reach as high as 40 and as low as zero in the same day. Skiing everywhere is generally great.

Stanley and the Sawtooth Mountains

A 45-minute drive north on Highway 75 will take you to the Sawtooth Observation area just over Galena Summit. On a sunny winter or summer day, you should definitely grab the camera and take this drive. If you choose, you can continue over the pass into the Sawtooth Basin and on to Stanley.

Stanley is known as the Gateway to the Salmon River and Sawtooth Mountains. It is a small town with dirt streets and rustic log cabins on the edge of the Sawtooth Mountains approximately 1 1/2 hours north of Ketchum on Highway 75. It has a small town atmosphere and amenities. During the winter, the people that go here are mainly snowmobilers, locals and backcountry enthusiasts. It is consistently one of the coldest places in Idaho during the winter months, but also one of the most beautiful. A day trip worth taking in any season.

The oval shaped Sawtooth Mountain range is 32 miles long, 20 miles wide and has 33 peaks over 10,000 feet. Thompson Peak is the highest measuring in at 10,751 feet and is located in the northern section of the range just north of Mt. Heyburn and directly behind the Stanley Ranger Station. The Sawtooth Mountains are located within the confines of the SNRA (Sawtooth National Recreational Area), which is a federally protected area consisting of 217,000 acres of wilderness where no motorized vehicles are allowed year round.

Before the 1800's, Sheepeater Indians were the only inhabitants of the Stanley Basin, surviving by hunting big game and fishing for the then-abundant salmon in the aptly named Salmon River. It wasn't until the fall of 1824 that a gentleman named Alexander Ross "discovered" the pristine Sawtooth Valley. What he discovered was that the Sawtooths were not only filled with beauty, they were bounding with fortunes of gold and silver. By the 1860's miners were swarming to the area in hopes of filling their pockets and feeding their families. Ten years later they had built up close to ten boomtowns in the Wood River and Sawtooth Valleys. By 1879 the Sheepeater Indians were run out and moved to reservations from the homeland they were trying to protect and exist in peacefully. By early 1900's, the miners were gone, the towns vacated, and the land forever scarred.

Remnants of these mining towns are still visible in many areas, from old roads jutting up the sides of mountains to entire towns and dredging equipment left in place. Please don't remove any artifacts from any of the mining townsites, as it is our history. Sad as it may be, it does need to be preserved.

Miners Cabin - The McBob Collection

Scenic Vistas

Galena Summit observation area is a 45-minute drive north of Ketchum on Highway 75. From the observatory pullout you can see the entire Sawtooth Mountain range, the headwaters of the historic Salmon River and the Stanley Basin. You want a phenomenal sunset any time of year? This is definitely the place.

Trail Creek Summit is located just 12 miles east of Ketchum on Trail Creek Road. From Ketchum, drive east on Sun Valley Road through the stop light and past the Sun Valley Lodge up the road to the summit. The final five miles are along a steep drop-off and skinny gravel road. Don't attempt this drive in a low-rider or car with bald tires. The rocks are quite sharp. Once at the top, the views back down the valley toward the Wood River Valley are exceptional. This is a summer-only road.

Bald Mountain is the main ski area located in Ketchum. A view from the top of this mountain is simply breathtaking. In either summer or winter you can take a chairlift ride to the top for a nominal fee and enjoy the views and get a bite to eat at the Lookout Lodge. When you've had enough and are out of film you can either ride the chairlift back down or, during the summer months, you can hike down the mountain on a single-track trail to the base of River Run. See the Mountain Biking section for more details.

Dollarhide Summit gives incredible views of the Pioneer and Smokey Mountains. This scenic summit is located approximately 24 miles out Warm Springs Road from Ketchum. After 12 miles you'll pass some hot springs on the side of Warm Springs Creek. The entire drive is gorgeous especially if you have time to continue driving over the summit to either Fairfield or Featherville and eventually to Highway 21 and back to the Wood River Valley for a full day of fun. This is a summer-only road and a detailed road map should be consulted first.

Proctor Mountain is a fun hike for the entire family, which begins at Trail Creek Cabin. From Ketchum, drive east on Sun Valley Road past the Sun Valley Lodge and mall area approximately 3 miles and turn right where the sign indicates "Trail Creek Cabin." Park here and walk through the grassy area behind the cabin, over the wooden bridge to the fenced area, follow the jeep trail along the left fence and up the hill. Next, take your first right and follow the trail up and up and up around the hill to the top of Proctor Mountain for incredible views of the Wood River Valley. Follow the main trail and make a loop out of it for about five miles total. Directly south of Proctor Mountain is Ruud Mountain, site of the first motorized chair lift of its type in Sun Valley and North America.

Moon over the Smokys - The McBob Collection

Lodging Guide

The thing to remember about lodging in the Sun Valley area is that it is a resort town, which means there is a wide variety of lodging available. We'll break it down for you here, but please remember prices and accommodations can and do change.

Hotel/Motel

1. Airport Inn - 820 S 4th, Hailey (208) 788-2477, Email: bookings@micron.net, web: taylorhotelgroup.com, $68 - $75, basic units, hot tub, kitchens, A/C, in Hailey.

2. Bald Mountain Lodge - 151 S Main, Ketchum (208) 726-9963 / (800) 892-7407, $45 - $95, kitchens, in-town location, fun place. This is a classic local landmark and a fun place to stay. Email: baldmt@svidaho.net.

3. Christiania - 651 Sun Valley Rd, Ketchum (208) 726-3351 / (800) 535-3241, $69 - $99, basic hotel, pool, hot tub, kitchens, fireplaces, in Ketchum. Email: christianialodge@sunvalley.net.

4. Clarion Inn - 600 N Main, Ketchum (208) 726-5900 / (800) 262-4833, $80 - $120, a nice place just north of downtown Ketchum, pool, hot tub, fireplaces, A/C. Web: svliving.com/clarionsunvalley.

5. Hailey Hotel - 201 S Main, Hailey (208) 788-3140, $30 - $35, basic units in downtown Hailey.

6. Heidelberg Inn - 1908 Warm Springs Rd, Ketchum (208) 726-5361 / (800) 284-4863, Email: bookings@micron.net, Web: taylorhotelgroup.com, $65 - $165, basic units, hot tub, pool, kitchens, fireplaces, near Warm Springs lifts.

7. High Country Motel - 765 S Main, Bellevue (208) 788-2050 / (800) 692-2050, $60 - $70, basic units, south valley location in Bellevue.

8. Hitchrack Motel - 619 S. Main, Hailey (208) 788-1696, $26 - $49, very basic.

9. Kentwood Lodge - 180 S Main, Ketchum (208) 726-4114 / (800) 805-1001, $79 - $129, nice hotel, pool, hot tub, kitchens, fireplaces, A/C, in Ketchum. Web: bestwestern.com.

10. Ketchum Korral Motor Lodge - 310 S Main, Ketchum (208) 726-3510 / (800) 657-2657, $45 - $105, hot tub, kitchens, fireplaces, another fixture and classic local landmark in Ketchum.

11. Lift Tower Lodge - 703 S Main, Ketchum (208) 726-5163 / (800) 462-8646, $42 - $80, basic units, south of Ketchum downtown, hot tub. This is another classic local landmark with an actual lift tower and chair in front. Email: imre@micron.net, web: vestra.net/lifttowerlodge.

12. Pennay's at River Run - West Ketchum (208) 726-9086 / (800) 736-7503, $125 - $335, located very close to the River Run lifts. Email: pennays@micron.net, web: pennays-sunvalley.com

13. Ski View Lodge - 409 S Main, Ketchum (208) 726-3441, $40 - $70, kitchens, another classic Ketchum landmark.

14. Tamarack Lodge - Sun Valley Rd & Walnut Ave, Ketchum (208) 726-3344 / (800) 521-5379, $69 - $124, great location in downtown Ketchum, hot tub, small kitchens, pool, fireplaces and A/C.

15. Tyrolean Lodge - 260 Cottonwood, Ketchum (208) 726-5336 / (800) 333-7912, $65 - $160, classic place, free continental breakfast, wet bars, pool, hot tub, in Ketchum and very close to the River Run lifts. Email: bookings@micron.net, web: taylorhotelgroup.com,

16. Wood River Inn - 601 N Main, Hailey (208) 578-0600 / (877) 542-0600, $69 - $125, pool, hot tub, fireplaces, free continental breakfast. This is the newest addition to the valley.

Resorts

17. Elkhorn Resort of Sun Valley - Elkhorn Village, Sun Valley (208) 622-4511 / (800) 355-4676, prices vary depending on whether you are in an outlying condo, in the village, or in the main hotel. All amenities are available: pool, spa, tennis, golf, shopping, etc.

18. Sun Valley Company - Sun Valley Village, Sun Valley (208) 622-4111 / (800) 786-8259, prices vary depending on whether you are in an outlying condo, in the village, or in one of the hotels. All amenities are available: pool, spa, tennis, golf, shopping, etc. Sun Valley is a world-class resort, and if you are not staying here it is definitely worth a stop to check it out.

Bed & Breakfasts

19. Idaho Country Inn - 134 Latigo Lane, Ketchum (208) 726-1019 / (800) 250-8341, $105 - $185 (seasonal), price includes hot tub and full breakfast. This is a charming log structure with rooms decorated in themes and provide great views. Email: idahoinn@magicline.com.

20. Knob Hill Inn - N Main St, Ketchum (208) 726-8010 / (800) 526-8010, $89 - $350 (seasonal), price includes use of the facilities including a fitness room, pool, hot tub, sauna, golf, etc., and also offers two restaurants. This is a huge inn with a Swiss motif. Another place to stop in and take a look if you're not staying here. Email: knobhillinn@sunvalley.net.

21. Povey Pensione - 128 W Bullion, Hailey (208) 788-4682 / (800) 370-4682, $65 year round, price includes a full breakfast. This is in a restored 100-year-old Victorian home in old Hailey. Email: tdavis11@sprynet.com. Web: virtualcities.com.

22. River Street Inn - 100 River St W, Ketchum (208) 726-3611 / (888) 746-3611, $89 - $195, price includes full breakfast, private baths, Japanese soaking tubs. Email: riverst@sprynet.com, Web: home.sprynet.com/sprynet/riverst.

Campgrounds / RV's

23. Sun Valley RV Resort - Hwy 75, 1 mile south of Ketchum (208) 726-3429, $18.50 - $30, open year round, modern facilities, heated pool, hot tub, located on the Big Wood River. Email: bornhoft@sunvalley.com.

Property Management

Base Mountain Properties - 200 W River St #101, Ketchum (208) 726-5601 / (800) 521-2515, email: info@basemountain.com, web: basemountain.com.
High Country Property Rentals & Management - 180 East Ave in Ketchum (208) 726-1256 / (800) 726-7076
Premier Resorts Sun Valley - 333 S. Main St in Ketchum (208) 727-4000 / (800) 635-4444.

Lodging in Surrounding Areas

Beckwith's Lodge - Highway 75 in Lower Stanley (208) 939-8936
Creek Side Lodge - Highway 21 in Stanley, (800) 523-0733.
Danners Cabins - Highway 21 in Stanley, (208) 774-3539.
Idaho Rocky Mountain Ranch - south of Stanley on Highway 75, (208) 744-3544.
Jerry's Country Store and Motel - Highway 75 in Lower Stanley, (208) 774-3566.
Mountain Village Resort - Highway 21 in Stanley, (208) 774-3661 / (800) 843-5475.
Redfish Lake Lodge - 10 miles south of Stanley on Redfish Lake, (208) 774-3536.
Redwood Motel - Stanley, (208) 774-3531.
Sawtooth Hotel - West end of Main St in Stanley, (208) 774-9947.
Sessions Lodge - 13 miles south of Stanley on Highway 75, (208) 774-3366.
Smiley Creek Lodge - 24 miles south of Stanley on Highway 75, (208) 774-3547.
Stanley Outpost - Highway 21 in Stanley, (208) 774-3646.
Torrey's Burnt Creek Inn - 21 miles north of Stanley on Highway 75, (208) 838-2313.
Valley Creek Motel - Highway 21 in Stanley, (208) 774-3606.
Wild Horse Creek Ranch - 20 miles east of Sun Valley on Trail Creek Road, (208) 588-2575.
Woolley's Lodging - Highway 75 in Lower Stanley, (888) 258-8965.

Lodging Map - Ketchum

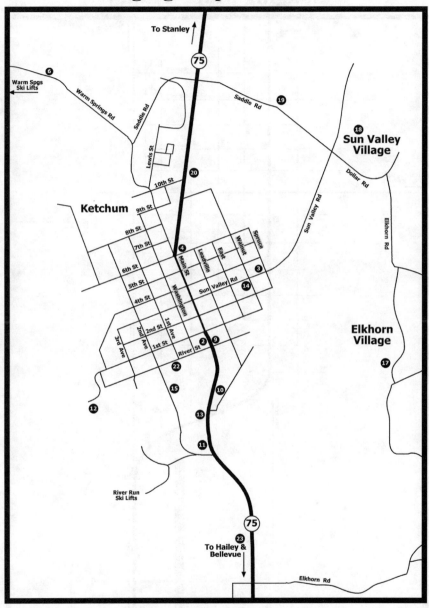

Lodging Map - Hailey

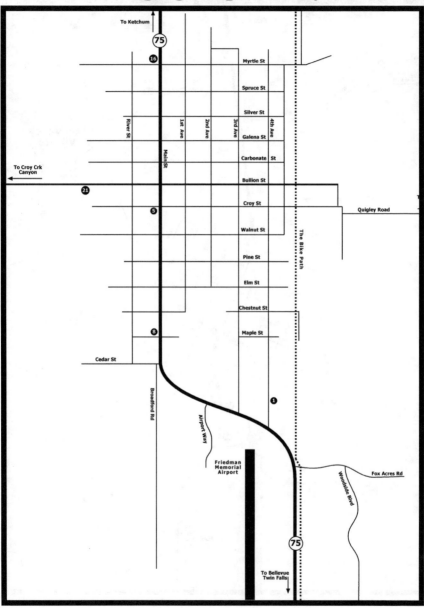

Bald Mountain Ski Area - The McBob Collection

Dining Guide

The local cuisine can give you a little taste of everything. There are world-class chefs and burger-throwing locals, but wherever you end up you are sure to have a meal to remember. The symbol "$" shows the price ranges from $ up to $$$, with $$$ being the most expensive. An asterisk (*) in front of a restaurant name means it is a recommended by the authors. Bellevue and other restaurants outside of the Ketchum/Hailey areas are not included on the maps.

Mexican
1. **KB's Burritos** 726-2232, corner of 6th & Washington Ave - Ketchum $
   When you're hungry, this is the place for great healthy food.
2. **La Nortenita** 788-1889, 321 S Main St - Bellevue $
   Truely authentic food in the south valley area.
*3. **Mama Inez** 726-4213, 7th St & Warm Springs Rd - Ketchum $
   Many locals favorite with a twist on traditional.
4. **Chapala's** 788-5065, 502 N Main St - Hailey $
   Hailey's local authentic Mexican food.
*5. **Desperado's** 726-3068, Corner of 4th & Washington Ave - Ketchum $
   Healthy food with killer homemade salsa and margaritas.
6. **Dos Amigos** 725-5001, 160 5th St - Ketchum $
   Off the beaten path, but promises a traditional Mexican meal.
7. **Joe's Southwestern Grill** 622-6424, Elkhorn Village Resort $$
   Located in Elkhorn, they have a good mix of southwestern food.
*8. **Viva Tacqueria** 788-4247, 411 N Main St - Hailey $
   Authentic nuevo Mexican food located in Hailey.

Italian
9. **Bob Dog's Pizza** 726-2358, Lower Giacobbi Square - Ketchum $
   Take-n-bake or slices to go, everything here is good.
10. **Clemente's** 788-1557, Alturas Plaza on E. Bullion St - Hailey $
   Traditional Italian everyday of the week.
11. **da Vinci's** 788-7699, 17 W. Bullion St - Hailey $$
   Classic Italian cuisine with nice atmosphere in Hailey.
12. **Il Giardino** 725-5730, 570 4th St - Ketchum $$
   Swiss French & Swiss Italian cuisine.
*13. **Il Naso** 726-7776, 5th & Washington Ave - Ketchum $$$
   The ultimate Italian fine dining experience.
14. **Piccolo** 726-9251, 220 East Ave - Ketchum $$
   Country-style Italian cuisine.
15. **Pizza Factory** 788-4100, 416 N Main St - Hailey $
   Good pizza at good prices located in Hailey.
16. **Rico's Pizza** 726-7426, 200 N Main St - Ketchum $
   Good pizza and ambiance all in one place.
*17. **Smoky Mountain Pizza** 622-5625, 200 Sun Valley Rd - Ketchum $
   Great food and fun!

18. South Valley Pizzeria 788-1456, Elm St - Bellevue $
    The south valley pizza stop with Take-n-Bake.
19. Stadium Pizza 788-1661, 315 S Main St - Hailey $
    Good pizza, good deck and TV's in Hailey.

Asian

20. China Pepper 726-0959, 511 Building on Leadville Ave - Ketchum $$
    Specialize in Thai, Szechwan and Hunan cuisine.
*21. Globus   726-1301, 6th & Main St - Ketchum $$
    Contemporary "large bowl" Thai dishes in a gourmet style.
*22. Omlay's   622-9333, 460 Washington Ave N - Ketchum $$
    Authentic cuisine in the heart of Ketchum
23. China Panda 726-3591, 515 N East Ave - Ketchum $
    Specialize in Hunan, Mandarin and Szechwan cuisine.
24. Can Tho   726-6207, 6th & Main St - Ketchum $
    Vietnamese and Thai cuisine, located in the train car.
25. Dawg Gone Good Teriyaki 725-0000, Giacobbi Square - Ketchum $
    Teriyaki vegetables and meats, quick and good.
26. Thai House 578-0777, 106 N Main St - Hailey $
    Authentic Thai cuisine in a local Hailey setting.
27. Sakura   788-9730, 731 N Main St - Hailey $$
    Good Japanese cuisine prepared in front of your eyes.
28. Sun Sushi 726-0959, 511 Building on Leadville Ave - Ketchum $$
    Fun place with good sushi inside China Pepper Restaurant.
*29. Sushi on Second 726-5181, 260 2nd St - Ketchum $$
    Great setting and food.

Continental

*30. Bellevue Bistro 788-5083, 620 S Main St - Bellevue $$
    Unique cuisine in a great setting in the south valley area.
31. Chandlers 726-1776, 200 S Main (Trail Creek Village) - Ketchum $$$
    Specialize in wild game and seafood.
32. Chi Chi's 788-4646, 721 N Main St - Hailey $
    Breakfast and lunch only at the north end of Hailey.
33. Cristina's 726-4499, 520 2nd St - Ketchum $$
    Great food, great deck and pastries to die for.
34. Evergreen 726-3888, Corner of River St & 1st Ave - Ketchum $$$
    Great meals in a rich, elegant atmosphere.
35. Full Moon Steak House 788-5912, 118 S Main St - Bellevue $$
    A good place for steaks...obviously
36. Felix's   726-1166, 960 N Main St (Knob Hill Inn) - Ketchum $$$
    A dinner-only mediterranean and continental cuisine.
*37. Galena Lodge 726-4010, located 25 miles north of Ketchum $$
    Great lunches and dinners served in a remote nordic lodge.

38. Gretchen's 622-2144, located in the Sun Valley Lodge $$
     The quick place to dine when staying at the Lodge.
39. Jesse's 622-4533, Elkhorn Village $$
     Specializes in meat and seafood with a large salad bar.
*40. Ketchum Grill 726-4660, East Ave & 5th St - Ketchum $$
     A fresh nuevo American menu with Idaho specialties.
41. Michel's Christiania 726-3388, Sun Valley Rd - Ketchum $$$
     Specialize in French cuisine in the historic Olympic Bar.
42. Ore House 726-2267, Main St - Ketchum $$
     Specialize in steaks, seafood and a large salad bar.
43. Otter's 726-6837, 180 6th St - Ketchum $$
     American cuisine with a flair from the Pacific Northwest.
44. The Konditorei 622-2235, Sun Valley Village $$
     Good food with a European twist in the Sun Valley Village.
45. Lodge Dining Room 622-2150, Sun Valley Lodge $$$
     Fine dining in historic lodge with great Sunday brunches.
*46. Pioneer Saloon 726-3139, 308 Main St N - Ketchum $$
     The ultimate prime-rib spot in town with historical decor.
47. Ram Restaurant 622-2225, Sun Valley Village $$$
     Specializes in wild game, etc. with live music.
*48. Redfish Lake Lodge 774-3536, 10 miles south of Stanley at the lake. $$
     A dining room, a bar, and views of the Sawtooths at sunset.
49. Sawtooth Club 726-5233, Main St - Ketchum $$
     Dining upstairs, bar downstairs and good food all the time.
50. Smiley Creek Lodge 774-3547, 37 miles north of Ketchum $
     Good food anytime located in the heart of the Sawtooths.
51. Soupcon 726-5034, 231 1/2 Leadville Ave - Ketchum $$$
     A delightful treat for yourself, get reservations.
52. Stock Pot 726-7733, 4th St & Main St - Ketchum $
     A good basic soup/salad combo meal anytime.
53. Trail Creek Cabin 622-2135, 4 mi. E of Ketchum on Sun Valley Rd $$
     Food with a western flair. Get there by sleigh or wagon.
54. Warm Springs Ranch 726-2609, Warm Springs Rd - Ketchum $$
     Steaks, seafood, lamb and scones to die for.
55. The Wild Radish 726-8468, 200 S Main-Trail Creek Village-Ketchum
     Good food in a great Hungarian style. $$$

Deli/Bakery Style

56. Perry's 726-7703, located 1 blk N of the Post Office - Ketchum $
     Deli-style food with great salads.
57. Cottonwood Cafe 726-0606, 411 5th St E - Ketchum $
     Good unique food located behind Giacobbi Square.
*58. Big Wood Bread 726-2034, 270 Northwood Way - Ketchum $
     Amazing soups and breads, located in the industrial area.

Breakfast/Lunch Only

*59. The Kneadery 726-9462, 260 Leadville - Ketchum $
     The breakfast only must-go place in Ketchum.

60. Knob Hill Inn Cafe 726-8010, 960 N Main St - Ketchum $$
     Breakfast only with Euro-style baked goods.

61. Esta   726-1668, 180 S Main St - Ketchum $
     Breakfast/ Lunch only with a unique cuisine.

62. Buckin' Bagel 726-8256, 200 1st Ave - Ketchum $
     Bagel and sandwiches to die for.

Pub & Casual Dining

63. Red Elephant Saloon 788-6047, 107 S Main St - Hailey $
     A bar with a dining room and food 'til midnight.

64. Apple's Bar & Grill 726-7067, Base of Warm Springs - Ketchum $
     Apre-ski extraordinaire. Burgers and beer.

65. Baldy Base Club 726-3838, Base of Warm Springs - Ketchum $$
     Apre-ski with all kinds of food to choose from. Full Bar.

*66. Cafe at the Brewery 788-0805, 202 N Main St - Hailey $$
     Wonderful brewpub style food.

67. Roosevelt Grill 726-0051, Main St & Sun Valley Rd - Ketchum $$
     Brewpub style food with live music all the time.

68. Whiskey Jacques 726-3200, 251 N Main St - Ketchum $
     The place you'll end up while out on the town any night.

Burgers, Etc.

*69. Grumpy's No Phone, 860 Warm Springs Rd - Ketchum $
     A must do! Huge beers, killer burgers and fowl-burgers.

70. Lefty's Bar & Grill 726-2744, 213 6th St E - Ketchum $
     Casual bar atmosphere with a pool table and TV's.

71. Hot Dog Adventure Co. 726-0117, Next to Casino Club - Ketchum $
     If you want a good wiener, just kidding. Good food on Main.

*72. Sub Shack 725-SUBS, 371 Washington Ave - Ketchum $
     Excellent subs on homemade bread. Go there!

*73. The Wicked Spud 788-0009, 305 N Main St - Hailey $
     Hailey will never be the same...burgers and beer Hailey-style.

Wine Bars

*74. Sun Valley Wine Co 726-2442, 360 Leadville Ave N - Ketchum $$
     Endless wine choices and a great place to start the evening.

75. The Galleria Wine & Espresso Bar 726-1707, Galleria Mall-Ketchum
     Small, quiet and a nice place to chill out. $$

Juice Bars

*76. Akasha Organics In the Chapter One Bookstore - Ketchum $
     Outstanding natural foods and fresh organic juices.

Dining Map - Ketchum

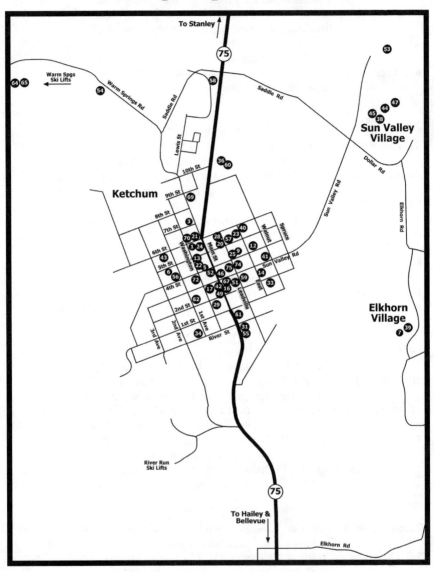

Dining Map - Hailey

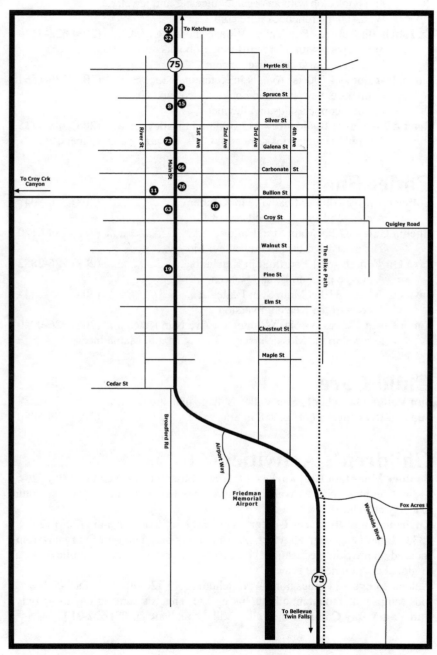

Bookstores

Chapter One Bookstore - 160 N Main St in Ketchum.......... (208) 726-5425
  Fun bookshop with an organic juice bar and jewelry.
  Web: chapteronebookstore.com
Ex Libris Bookstore - Sun Valley Village shopping area....... (208) 622-8174
  Small space with a large offering of books.
  Email: exlibris@compuserve.com
Iconoclast Books - 100 1st Ave. N in Ketchum...................... (208) 726-1564
  Many rare, new and used books, videos and CD's.
  Email: iconoclast@sunvalley.net
Read All About It Bookstore - 312 S Main in Hailey............ (208) 788-1415
  The only Hailey bookstore with CD's, magazines, newpapers, etc.

Coffee Shops

Coffee Grinder - 4th & Leadville in Ketchum...................... (208) 726-8048
  A classic place for a good cup of Joe.
Cucina Cafe - 620 N Main St in Hailey.................................. (208) 788-6120
  The only drive-thru in the valley! Finally...
Java On Fourth - 191 Fourth St in Ketchum......................... (208) 726-2882
  A classic place to go and be seen.
Java On Main - 310 N Main St in Hailey.............................. (208) 788-2444
  A copy of the Ketchum version.
Terra Cotta Espresso - 680 Washington Ave N in Ketchum. (208) 726-0949
  Located in the Moss Nursery building next to Mama Inez.

Child Care

Sun Valley Playschool - Sun Valley Village mall area........... (208) 622-2288
Super Sitters Inc. - PO Box 988 in Sun Valley...................... (208) 788-5080

Children's Activities

Boulder Mountain Clayworks - 491 Tenth Street #B-6 Ketchum (208) 726-4484. Children's classes available in throwing, handbuilding and clay sculpture in a clay arts studio.
Environmental Resource Center - 411 East 6th Street Ketchum (208) 726-4333. Email: erc@sunvalley.net. A community based non-profit organization focused on providing educational programs and resources to the public on local to global environmental issues.
Galena Lodge - 24 miles north of Ketchum (208) 726-4010. Offer 3-5 day kids camps with mountain biking, hiking, etc. This is a summer day camp only.
Sun Valley Day Camp - Sun Valley Village mall area (208) 622-2133.

Fitness Centers

Blaine County Fitness Center - 21 E. Maple in Hailey (208) 788-2124. They have a very small gym with just the basics. Open to the general public.
The Rock Down Under Climbing Gym - 21 E. Maple in Hailey (208) 788-1155. Located in the basement of the Blaine County Fitness Center.
Sun Valley Athletic Club - 131 First Ave in Ketchum (208) 726-3664. A serious workout facility with many machines, free weights, aerobics, pool, jacuzzi and sauna.

Galleries

Ketchum has a large amount of art galleries carrying everything from fine art to southwestern jewelry to Southeast Asian collectibles. They are scattered around the main downtown Ketchum area. During the summer and winter months, Gallery Walks are hosted once a month. Check local newspapers for dates and locations.

Libraries

Bellevue Public Library - 115 E Pine in Bellevue.................. (208) 788-2128
Community Library - 415 Spruce Ave N in Ketchum............ (208) 726-3493
Hailey Public Library - 7 Croy St in Hailey............................ (208) 788-2036

Museums

Bellevue Old City Hall Museum - 209 N Main in Bellevue... (208) 788-2128
Blaine County Historical Museum - 118 N Main in Hailey... (208) 788-1801
Ketchum/Sun Valley Heritage & Ski Museum -
Corner of Washington Ave and 1st St in Ketchum.................... (208) 726-8118
Ore Wagon Museum - 5th & East Ave. in Ketchum................No Phone
Sun Valley Center for Arts - 191 5th St E in Ketchum.......... (208) 726-9491
Email: svcenter@micron.net, Web: sunvalleyid.com/svcenter

Theatres - Movie

Liberty Theatre - 110 N Main in Hailey................................ (208) 788-3300
Magic Lantern - 1st Ave & 2nd St in Ketchum..................... (208) 726-4274
Ski Time Cinemas - 1st Ave & 2nd St in Ketchum................ (208) 726-1039
Sun Valley Opera House - Sun Valley Village...................... (208) 622-2244

Yoga / Massage / Day Spas

The Sacred Cow - 215 Northwood Way #J Ketchum............. (208) 726-7018
Solavie Day Spa & Salon - 511 Leadville Ketchum................(208) 726-7211
Salon Gamine - 333 S. Main Ketchum................................... (208) 726-4540

What to do with your pet?

Ketchum is a very dog-friendly town. Some tend to think there are more dogs than people, although this is not true, the question of what to do with Fido can arise.

Any trail, either in the mountains or in town is great for dogs. The same goes for the winter with the exception of some of the nordic skiing trails. See the Nordic Skiing section for details on skiing with your dogs. There are some obvious things to do with your pet: Always keep them on a leash or in voice control. Clean up after them when around town or on someone's lawn. Don't beat your dog or one of the many animal-lovers in town will kick your ass. Don't keep them locked up in a closed car. If your dog is a senseless barker then shut them up. No one likes a dog who is tied up to a tree barking. I have seen many dogs set "free" of their leash just to shut them up. Please be a responsible animal person. See the phone book for a list of kennels.

City Parks

In addition to our expansive natural playground, we have city parks too! They provide space for our great team sports such as soccer, ultimate Frisbee and softball. They also offer you a place to lay around and enjoy the sunshine.

Ketchum
Atkinson Park - located just off Third Ave behind Hemingway Elementary School.
Hailey
Hop Porter City Park - located east of downtown on Bullion Street.
Lions Park - located east of downtown on Bullion Street just over the river.
L. Heagle - located in the Della View subdivision southwest of downtown on War Eagle Drive.
Roberta McKercher City Park - located at the south end of Third and Fourth Avenue next to the Armory Bldg.
Deerfield Park - located in the Deerfield subdivision east of downtown on East Ridge Drive.
Curtis Park - located directly east of downtown at the end of Bullion Street.

Rainy Day Activities

The kids say Mexico would have been the better choice for a vacation and your spouse is, well let's just say things are gray and gloomy. What to do??

Get a video, go to the movies, go bowling in the basement of the Sun Valley Lodge, visit a museum, go shopping, bar-hop, hit some of the galleries, have a contest to see who can fill up their mouth with rain drops first, jump in mud-puddles, watch the Big Wood River go over its banks, surf the internet, play rock-paper-scissors, indian leg-wrestling (my brother will kick your butt), get a massage, give your spouse a massage, go to a bar and give someone a massage, workout at one of the health clubs, act like you have serious money and go look at real estate, test drive some new cars, go to the Duchin Room and listen to Joe play the piano, go drink tons of coffee and start at the top of this list. Have fun, the rains don't last for too long but bad attitudes do, make the most of it and be creative.

Calendar of Events

The Wood River and Sawtooth Valleys have a constant flow of events happening throughout the year. If there's not a concert happening, then there is wine tasting and an antique show. We won't disappoint you without anything to do.
Below is a typical calendar of events for the valley. For specific times and dates, call the local Chamber of Commerce located at the front of this guidebook.

January
>Ski The Rails: a nordic ski tour from Ketchum to Hailey.

February
>Boulder Mountain Tour: 32k nordic ski race.
>Valentine's Music Concert in Ketchum.

March
>Paw & Pole Nordic Ski Race: For you and your animal.
>Sun Valley Gourmet Nordic Ski Tour.
>Sun Valley Pro-Am Classic.

April
>Bald Mountain Ski Area closes: huge party weekend.
>Nordic Ski Trails close for the season.

May
>Twilight Jazz Series begins and goes through September.
>Jazz on the Green begins and goes through September.
>Art Gallery Walks begin and continue through September.

June
>Elkhorn Resort begins Summer Concert Series.
>Women's international bike race ends in Ketchum.
>Sun Valley Ice Shows begin and continue through September.

July
>Tour & Parade of Homes.
>Fourth of July Parade and local town celebrations.
>Sun Valley Summer Symphony begins.
>Antique Fairs around the Wood River and Sawtooth valleys.
>Backcountry Trail Run.
>Chamber Music Concert.

August
>Sun Valley Arts & Crafts Festival.
>Northern Rockies Folk Festival.
>Chamber Music Concert.
>Sun Valley Wine Auction.
>Danny Thompson Memorial Golf Tournament.

September
>Ketchum Wagon Days Celebration & Parade.

October
>Swing n' Dixie Jazz Jamboree in Ketchum.

November
>Bald Mountain Ski Area opens.

December
>Winterstart nordic ski race.
>Lakecreek Relay nordic ski race.

Your Own Private Idaho - The McBob Collection

The Summer Guide

There are those who consider summertime to be the jewel of Sun Valley. We have some of the most incredible mountain beauty one could possibly imagine. Mountain peaks with giant summer snowfields dropping into high alpine lakes so deep blue in color you become lost in thought, and wildflowers so colorful and fragrant you'll never want to go home. In fact, most of the residents of the Sun Valley area did just that. Ask any local and they'll tell you their story of visiting the area and never leaving. Come and enjoy our version of Paradise.

Activities are listed A - Z

ATV Tours

We've all been there before. You are just about at your high point of the hike and the mountains are coming into full view when all of the sudden you hear the roar of a four-stroke engine coming up behind you. It may seem like such a silly thing to be in a pristine mountain setting, blasting your way up a valley into the wilderness somewhere on an ATV (all-terrain vehicle). However, for some people this is the only way they are ever going to see such beauty due to physical limitations. For others it's just a fun thing to do.

The USFS has regulations on which trails can be used for ATV's by posting signs at trailheads. If you have any questions on where to ride your own ATV give them a call. The USFS phone numbers are located at the front of this guidebook. For locally operated ATV tours up to the Boulder Mountains, we have one outfitter who makes a great adventure of it.

ATV Tour Companies
Mulligan's Sun Valley Adventures - PO Box 381 Sun Valley (208) 726-9137.

Cruising through the Boulder Mountains - Courtesy Mulligan's Sun Valley Adventures

Air Charters / Sightseeing Tours

The mountain scenery around the Sun Valley area is truly amazing. We have over five different mountain ranges including the famous Sawtooths near Stanley. Seeing it all from the air is quite an experience. There are countless mountain lakes, snowfields, mountain summits and wildlife to view. After a flight around the area, your appreciation for this part of Idaho will certainly grow.

There are many companies offering sightseeing tours and air charter service. The air charters are popular for people flying into the Middle Fork of the Salmon River, as well as those people who need to get to the more remote areas of the region. Give any of them a call and go check out the area.

Air Charter/Sightseeing Companies

Access Air - 800-307-4984 web: access-air.com
Air Ketchum - (888) 701-2494 web: airketchum.com
McCall & Wilderness Air - (800) 992-6559 web: flying@mccallair.com
Pere-air Aircraft Charters - (208) 788-9134 web: pere-air.com
SessAir - (208) 622-7522.
Stanley Air Taxi - (208) 774-2276 / (800) 225-2236
email: diat@ruralnetwork.net
web: ecoguild.com/website-index/friends/stanley-airtaxi/default.htm

Pettit Lake and the Sawtooth Mountains by Air - The McBob Collection

Backpacking

If you have ever been backpacking in paradise, then you've obviously been back-packing around Sun Valley. Amongst the five mountain ranges close to town, you will find beautifully maintained trails, wilderness areas where only foot traf-fic is possible, pristine mountain lakes, high snowfields, an abundance of wildlife and very few people.

As the Sun Valley area becomes more popular, people tend to congre-gate at the trailheads close to town. Keep in mind, the further you get away from town, the more you'll end up enjoying the experience all the better. Just about any valley outside of town leads to your own private Idaho.

By early of July most of the high trails are open, but check in with local shops or the USFS when in doubt. There are a few local guidebooks which cover the backpacking possibilities in greater detail. These guidebooks are available at most outdoor stores as well as local bookstores.

On the map on the following page is a number which shows trailhead access for the backpacking areas we recommend.

Recommendations

Pioneer Mountains
1. Kane Lake - Drive approximately 20 miles east on Sun Valley Road to Trail Creek Road and over Trail Creek Summit to the turn off approximately 7.5 miles later. Turn right and continue about 5 miles to the trailhead. It is around 3 miles one-way to the lake.
2. Pioneer Cabin - There are four different ways to get to Pioneer Cabin, of the four, the one we recommend is very scenic. Drive approximately five miles south of Ketchum to East Fork Road and continue through the tiny town of Triumph for just over seven miles and turn left on Hyndman Creek Road. In just over 3 miles you'll reach the trailhead for Johnstone Creek. Park here and follow this trail up to the cabin for a great Pioneer Mountain hike. It is just over 5 miles to the cabin.

Whitecloud Mountains
3. Washington Lake - Drive approximately 15 miles south of Stanley to Fourth of July Creek Road, turn east and drive up another 10 miles to the trailhead. In 2.5 miles you'll reach Washington Lake and 9600' in elevation. Short, sweet and beautiful.

Sawtooth Mountains
4. Alice Lake - Drive 18 miles south of Stanley to the turn off for Petit Lake on the right. Continue to the parking lot on the north side of Pettit Lake, and follow the trail for 5.5 miles to Alice Lake. This trip is gorgeous.
5. Hell Roaring Lake - Drive about 15 miles south of Stanley and turn west on Road #210. Cross over the Salmon River and turn left on a very rough road to the trailhead in about 3.3 miles. From here it is 2 miles to the lake.

6. Cramer Lakes - From Stanley, drive 4 miles south on Highway 75 to Redfish Lake Road and drive to the lodge. Take the shuttle boat across the lake ($5) and from the boat landing follow the main trail through the camping area. It is just over 6.5 miles one-way to the first lake.

7. Sawtooth Lake - From Stanley, drive 2.5 miles west on Highway 21 to Iron Creek Road #619. Turn left here and continue 3 miles to the trailhead. From here it is just over 4 miles to the lake. Don't forget to take some food and water along.

Backpacking/Outdoor Stores

Backwoods Moutain Sports - Warm Springs Road & Hwy 75 in Ketchum (208) 726-8818

Elephants Perch - 220 E Sun Valley Rd Ketchum (208) 726-3497 web: elephantsperch.com, email: perchinfo@svidaho.net

Important Phone Numbers

Ketchum Ranger District - (208) 622-5371
Stanley Ranger District - (208) 774-3681
Sawtooth National Recreation Area - (208) 726-7672
Lost River Ranger District - (208) 588-2224
Yankee Fork Ranger District - (208) 838-2201
EMERGENCY 911

On the way to Alpine Lake - The McBob Collection

Backpacking Map

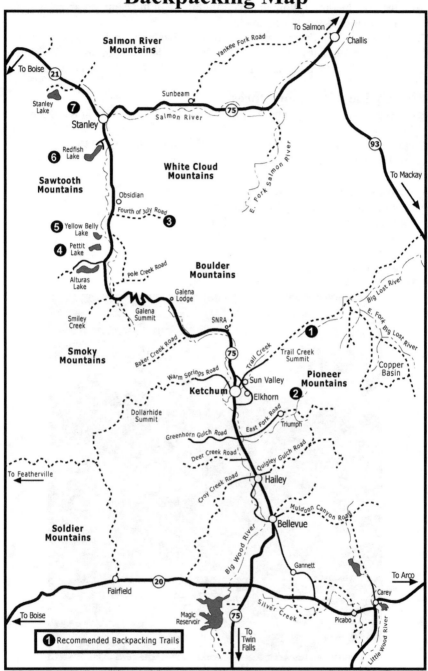

Mountain Biking

Sun Valley and mountain biking have become synonymous. Most of the mountain bike magazines write an article at least once a year about the magnitude of riding available here. Well, seeing is believing.

Sun Valley mountain biking has something for everyone. There are fun, easy jeep trails to gnarly single-track that would even make your grandmother sweat! However, every trail for mountain biking is also used for other sports, such as trail running, hiking, motorcycling, horseback riding, etc. So please use extreme caution when descending any trail and no matter what other rules say, just yield to everyone and everything.

More and more trails are being produced in the Sun Valley area each year through a combination of work from volunteers, local trail organizations, the BLM and the USFS. For details on the mountain bike trails listed below, pick up a copy of *Good Dirt*, the local mountain bike guidebook, which contains 70 rides. It is very detailed and gives great explanations of trails and maps. You can get a copy at any outdoor or bike shop in the area.

Most local shops will steer you to a quick, easily-accessible trailhead close to town especially if you are renting a bike from them. Try to make it out of the immediate area, even to the Stanley area, which has some of the best riding around. Most rides in the south Hailey areas open in early May, with most northern and Ketchum areas open by June...we hope.

*Note: Please do not ride on wet trails after rain, snow or early season, and please do not skid around corners. Help us preserve our trails.

Recommendations

Ketchum Area
1. Bald Mountain - The Sun Valley Company owns and operates the Bald Mountain Ski Area. They have created some spectacular single-track trails all around the mountain. You can either ride up and down, or take the chairlift to the top and have a phenomenal descent of 3250 feet. Start at either the River Run or Warm Springs side of the mountain on the edge of Ketchum.
2. Greenhorn Gulch - This area has a vast network of single-track trails. After a casual start to all the trails, they climb and loop back for a great downhill back to the parking lot. These trails are for the intermediate and advanced riders, and are located at the end of Greenhorn Gulch Road 6 miles south of Ketchum.
3. Corral Creek - A perfect beginner ride on single-track near the edge of town. Perfect for a quickie anytime of the day. Located 3 miles east of Sun Valley on Trail Creek Road.

Outlying Areas
4. Cove Creek - A great south-valley ride for the early mountain bike season giving exceptional views of the Pioneer and Boulder Mountains. Start in Quigley Canyon on the edge of Hailey and ride through the mountains to Triumph and back to Hailey via the Bike Path. Be prepared, it is a long, fun ride.

5. Galena Lodge - In the winter, this is a nordic center, and during the summer the jeep and single-track trails provide great riding possibilities. Don't miss out on a chance to ride here. Located 24 miles north of Ketchum on Highway 75.

Stanley Area
6. Redfish Lake to Decker Flats - An amazingly scenic ride for intermediate riders in the heart of the Sawtooth Mountains between Stanley and Galena Summit. Start riding at Redfish Lake, then down to the flats and back again. Fun!
7. Elk Mountain - On this ride you get some moderate climbing, incredible single-track, gorgeous meadows and wildlife. If you want views, this is the ride. Located 5 miles west of Stanley on Highway 21.

There are a few local touring companies offering hourly to multi-day rides. All are very respectable and have great guides. This is a fun way to go if you want the fun riding, great views and good food. There is also one mountain bike school, which is especially popular for those wanting to give the kids some fun away from the parents (or vice-versa) for a day or two.

Touring Companies/Schools
Trail Quest Mtn Bike School - PO Box 1028 Ketchum (208) 726-7401.
Sun Valley Single Track - PO Box 4663 Ketchum (208) 622-TOUR.
email: svbiketours@sunvalley.net, web: home.rmci.net/svbiketours
Venture Outdoors - PO Box 2251 Hailey (208) 788-5049 / 800-528-LAMA.
Email: venout@micron.net, web: ventureoutdoorsidaho.com.

Rental/Sales/Service
Backwoods Moutain Sports - Warm Springs Road & Hwy 75 in Ketchum (208) 726-8818.
Downhill Service - 1007 B Warm Springs Road Ketchum (208) 726-1825.
Durance Cycleworks - 131 Second St Ketchum (208) 726-7693.
email: durance@svidaho.net, web: durance.com
Elephants Perch - 220 E Sun Valley Rd Ketchum (208) 726-3497.
web: elephantsperch.com, email: perchinfo@svidaho.net
Formula Sports - 460 N Main Ketchum (208) 726-3194.
Kelly Sports - Colonnade Building Ketchum (208) 726-8503.
Pete Lanes - Sun Valley Road in Sun Valley (208) 622-2276.
Riverwear - Hwy 21 in Stanley (208) 774-3592.
Sawtooth Rentals - Hwy 75 in Stanley (208) 774-3409.
Ski-Tek - 191 Sun Valley Rd Ketchum (208) 726-7503.
web: ski-tek.com
Sturtos (Sturtevants) - 314 N. Main Ketchum (208) 726-4512.
Email: sturtos@micron.net , web: sturtos.com
Sturtevants - Hailey (208) 788-7847.
Sun Summit Ski & Cycle - 791 Warm Springs Rd Ketchum (208) 726-0707.
Sun Summit South - 507 S Main Hailey (208) 788-6006.
True Wheel - 400 N Main Hailey (208) 788-5433.

Mountain Bike Map

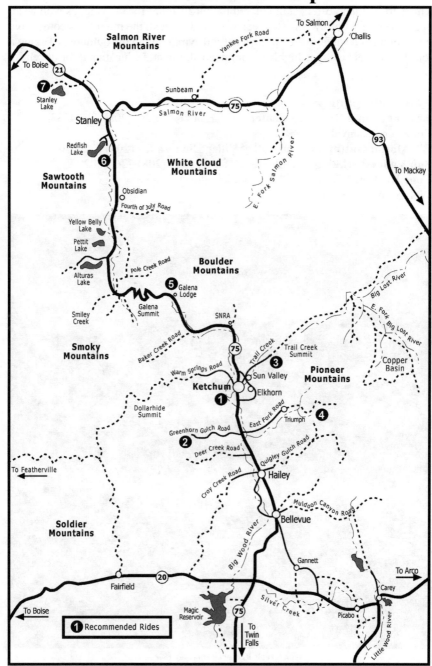

41

Bird & Wildflower Tours

This part of Idaho offers some incredible bird habitat for viewing, as well as an abundance of wildflowers. Between May and August, the mountains come alive with colors and songbirds creating a natural symphony in the outdoors. Taking a tour to see this beauty is highly recommended, fun and educational for the entire family.

Tour Companies
Environmental Resource Center - 411 E 6th Ketchum (208) 726-4333
Email: erc@sunvalley.net
Bill Mason Outfitters - Sun Valley Village Sun Valley (208) 622-9305
Sun Valley Trekking - PO Box 2200 Sun Valley (208) 726-1002
Tour Du Jour - PO Box 581 Sun Valley (208) 788-3903
Web: webpak.net/~trdjr

Silver Creek Preserve - Courtesy Tour du Jour

Camping

The Sawtooth National Recreation Area (SNRA) has well over 700 campsites from south of Ketchum up through the Stanley area. The campsites are developed with all the amenities such as picnic tables, fire-rings, restrooms, water, etc. (**Hint:** On the busier weekends of the summer and fall, these sites can go fast leaving you high and dry looking for somewhere to slumber.)

If you are not into crowds, a bit more adventurous and self-contained, there are many primitive campsites. Most dirt roads (unless labeled as private) lead to some sort of a primitive campsite. We have recommended several campgrounds throughout the area, however, there are many more campgrounds in the area than are labeled on the map.

The SNRA headquarters is a funky looking building (a manufactured mountain look-alike) about 8 miles north of Ketchum on Hwy 75. The friendly staff there can easily tell you where the crowds and wildlife are and what to expect in certain areas.

Most campgrounds are open by Memorial Day and close around the middle of October. The time limit for camping is 14 days maximum at any given campground. The USFS rangers will be more than happy to enforce your departure should you go beyond that time limit.

Camping Etiquette:

1. Garbage will happen, therefore, if you take it in there, take it out with you. Most campgrounds provide garbage receptacles, aside from the primitive ones, so please use them.

2. The restroom is the place if you need to relieve yourself. Hold your breath and use it. If one is not provided, go at least 200 feet from any water source and dig a hole 6 inches deep. When finished, take the toilet paper with you and throw it away. Do not burn it or leave it on the surface of the soil.

3. Water is precious in campgrounds. Do not pour food or human waste in a water source. For your gray (kitchen) water, go at least 200 feet from the nearest water source. If you pollute the water, think about what the upstream campers could be doing to your drinking water.

4. Campfires are a luxury item. Treat them that way. Since wood is getting scarce in certain campgrounds, please refrain from making a campfire until evenings unless it is truly necessary. If you make a campfire just for the enjoyment of smelling burning wood, become a firefighter.

5. Do you like people in your face taking your photo? Do you like four-wheel drive vehicles chasing you down? Do you like people yelling at you? No? I didn't think so. That's enough said on how to act around the wildlife.

6. Please be responsible campers and treat your campground and the land as if you were your own home.

On the map on the following page is a picture of a "tent" showing campsites around the area. Most of the sites are quite obvious. Please respect private property and USFS regulations.

Recommendations

Ketchum Area
1. North Fork of Big Wood River - Drive about 8 miles north of Ketchum on Hwy 75 to the SNRA headquarters building and turn right. Go straight up the road past the building to find all kinds of campsites.
2. Trail Creek Area - Drive 12.5 miles east from Ketchum past Sun Valley Resort and up over Trail Creek Summit. This gorgeous valley has many developed and primitive sites. The road to the summit is rough, rocky and dusty.

Galena Area
3. Prairie Creek - Drive north of Ketchum on Highway 75 for 18.5 miles to Prairie Creek Road and turn left. There are several primitive sites along the three miles to the trailhead and turn-around area.

Stanley/Sawtooth Basin
4. Chemeketan - 34.5 miles north of Ketchum on Highway 75, or 27 miles south of Stanley brings you to Road #215. Turn south on it and in approximately 3 miles you reach a campground. This is the headwaters of the mighty Salmon River and a wonderful valley to explore. There are plenty of campsites here.
5. Alturas Lake - About 40.5 miles north of Ketchum on Highway 75, or just over 21 miles south of Stanley is Road #205. Turn west here and drive to any number of campgrounds around the lake. If it is a bit crowded there, any dirt road leading off the main road will get you to primitive camping.
6. Redfish Lake - Approximately 55 miles north of Ketchum on highway 75 and 4 miles south of Stanley takes you to Redfish Lake Road. If you don't mind crowds, boats, jetskis, etc, then this is the place for you. It is extremely beautiful here and the hiking/backpacking is phenomenal. Best bet is to come here in the day, avoid the crowds and camp elsewhere.

Camping/Outdoor Stores
Backwoods Moutain Sports - Warm Springs Road & Hwy 75 in Ketchum (208) 726-8818.
Chateau Drug - Giacobbi Square Ketchum (208) 726-5696.
Elephants Perch - 220 E Sun Valley Rd Ketchum (208) 726-3497.
web: elephantsperch.com, email: perchinfo@svidaho.net

Important Phone Numbers
Ketchum Ranger District - (208) 622-5371
Stanley Ranger District - (208) 774-3681
Sawtooth National Recreation Area - (208) 726-7672
Lost River Ranger District - (208) 588-2224
Yankee Fork Ranger District - (208) 838-2201
EMERGENCY 911

Camping Map

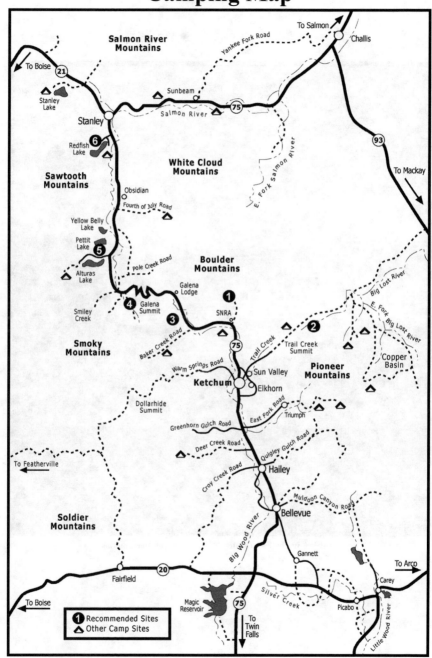

Climbing in the Sawtooths - Courtesy Sawtooth Mountain Guides

Climbing/Mountaineering

The Sawtooth Mountains offer the traditional alpine rock climber some of the best granite around. By using the word "alpine," I mean there is no sport climbing here. The Sawtooths offer long approaches, long routes and serious commitment. If you plan on climbing in the Sawtooths, please use extreme caution. Rockfall, lightning and other natural occurences can stop climbers in their tracks.

A rather large controversial issue is the use of bolts and fixed anchors in wilderness areas. The USFS has considered banning the use of bolts and other fixed anchor devices in areas across the country, and unfortunately, the Sawtooths have been put in the spotlight. If the USFS follows through with their ban, technical alpine rock climbing in the Sawtooths will come to an abrupt halt. Enjoy it while you can.

Routes can be found all over the Sawtooths, but the most abundant and technical are found on the Elephants Perch. A picture of the "Perch" is on page 5. It was named in the 1960's by a climbing group from the Iowa Mountaineers after making the first known ascent. To this day, climbers come to the Elephants Perch from all over the world to scale its pristine alpine granite walls. The local climbing shop in Ketchum has all the topos you need to get the beta on routes for the Elephants Perch and surrounding crags.

Access to the Elephants Perch is best done by taking a shuttle boat from Redfish Lake Lodge to the far end of the lake ($5). Follow the main trail from the boat dock up the canyon. After about 2.5 miles you will reach some granite slabs next to the creek, cross on the non-existent climber's trail and continue following it up to the slabs below the Perch. Be prepared to make a Tyrolean Traverse in early spring when the creek is flowing at dangerous levels.

Although there is no other developed rock climbing areas close to Sun Valley, we do have a top rope rock about 10 miles up Warm Springs Road with some nice hot springs next to it.

A professional guide service is operated out of Stanley, Sawtooth Mountain Guides. They know and work in the Sawtooths on a daily basis and are well worth the expense if you are interested in learning how to rock climb or if you want a guide for a day outing. They also offer avalanche courses in the winter.

Local Shops/Guides
Sawtooth Mountain Guides - P.O. Box 18 Stanley, ID 83278 (208) 774-3324
Email: getaway@sawtoothguides.com, web: sawtoothguides.com
Elephants Perch - 220 E Sun Valley Rd Ketchum (208) 726-3497.
web: elephantsperch.com, email: perchinfo@svidaho.net
Redfish Lake Lodge - PO Box 9 Stanley (208) 774-3536

Fishing

The Sun Valley area has some of the best fishing in the country. This means that on the busy holiday weekends the many mountain lakes and valley rivers can get a bit crowded making the bank real estate rather scarce. However, there are so many places to get away from crowds and into fish, with a little curiosity and back roads you should be able to find your own piece of paradise.

The Big Wood River and its tributaries offer some wonderful bait and fly-fishing possibilities, but access can be a problem. Therefore, please respect private property and only access the rivers where signs indicate it is possible.

The general fishing season runs from Memorial Day weekend to November 30th. However, the yearly spring mountain run-off has been known to hinder the fishing until Fourth of July weekend, so call ahead and be prepared for high water in early season. The steelhead run is in the Salmon River downstream from Stanley in the early spring, with only whitefish may be caught from December 1st through March 31st.

Any child 14 to 17 years old is required to purchase an Idaho State Fishing License, which costs $8. Non-resident children under the age of 14 must be accompanied by a licensed adult and their daily catch must be included in the license holder's daily limit. Non-resident adult licenses can be purchased in 1-day, 3-day, and 10-day or for the season ranging from $7 to $51. Idaho residents can purchase a full season license for $16. General fishing regulations, licenses and supplies can be purchased at any of the fishing stores in the area.

The Big Wood River is catch-and-release from just below Bellevue to the SNRA north of Ketchum. The same goes for the East Fork of the Big Lost River and downstream from the confluence. General rules apply above and below these points. Most all of the Salmon River drainage is catch-and-release. For more specific information pick up a copy of the rules and regulations in any shop.

Some of the fly shops in town hold free fly-fishing casting classes each week. Check the weekly calendar section in the *Idaho Mountain Express* newspaper for time and location of classes.

Being able to fish is a privilege, so please practice conservation everywhere you go. Please don't litter, but try to pick any extra garbage that might be around you. Our river and stream banks are very precious due to the erosion caused by the spring mountain run-off each year. Please tread lightly along the banks and try not to drive in and out of the streams just to get 10 feet closer to a fishing hole.

Most of the fishing stores in town offer guide services to some of the local spots and even a few secret ones. If you are unfamiliar with the area and only have a short period of time to fish in the valley, then I highly recommend the use of a guide. You will get into some fish, learn some technique and have great stories to tell everyone back home.

The map on the following page shows a picture of a "fish" indicating river/lake access for fishing. Most of the access is quite obvious, but when in doubt either ask someone or hire a local guide.

Recommended Fishing Areas

1. **Big Lost River** - Over Trail Creek Summit east of Sun Valley.
2. **Redfish Lake** - Over Galena Summit south of Stanley.
3. **Silver Creek** - South of Bellevue off Highway 20.
4. **The Salmon River** - North of Stanley all along Highway 75.

Guide Services

Bill Mason Outfitters - Sun Valley Village Sun Valley (208) 622-9305.
Lost River Outfitters - 171 N Main Ketchum (208) 726-1706.
email: lro@sunvalley.net, web: lostriveroutfitters.com
Silver Creek Outfitters - 500 N Main Ketchum (208) 726-5282.
email: silvercreek@flyshop.com, web: silver-creek.com
Venture Outdoors - PO Box 2251 Hailey (208) 788-5049 / 800-528-LAMA.
email: venout@micron.net, web: ventureoutdoorsidaho.com
Wood River Outfitters at Headwaters - 151 Main Ketchum (208) 726-5775.

Fishing Supply Shops

Bill Mason Outfitters - Sun Valley Village Sun Valley (208) 622-9305.
Bob's Sports - 12 W Bullion Hailey (208) 788-3308.
Chateau Drug - Giacobbi Square Ketchum (208) 726-5696.
Lost River Outfitters - 171 N Main Ketchum (208) 726-1706.
email: lro@sunvalley.net, web: lostriveroutfitters.com
McCoy's Tackle Shop - Ace of Diamond St Stanley (208) 774-3377.
Mountain Village Mercantile - Hwy 21 Stanley (208) 774-3507.
Silver Creek Outfitters - 500 N Main Ketchum (208) 726-5282.
email: silvercreek@flyshop.com, web: silver-creek.com
Silver Creek Supply - US Hwy 20 Picabo (208) 788-3536.
Sun Valley Outfitters - Elkhorn Village Elkhorn (208) 622-3400.
Wood River Outfitters at Headwaters - 151 Main Ketchum (208) 726-5775.

Andy McBob at Silver Creek - The McBob Collection

Fishing Map

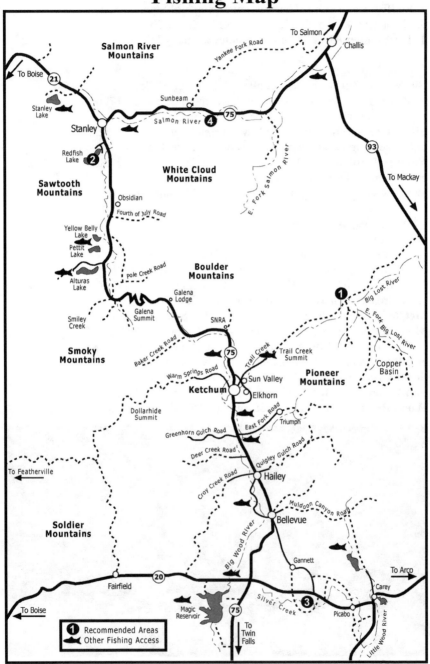

Golfing

Some people think of Sun Valley only for its skiing, but our world-class golf courses are a major attraction during summer months. With courses becoming clear of snow by early May, you can golf until your hands begin to freeze around the beginning of November.

The Sun Valley area has four public courses, Sun Valley, Elkhorn, Bigwood and Warm Springs. During the summer season tee times can be made as early as 7am and as late as 8pm. But always plan ahead and get reservations at anytime of the summer especially around the bigger holiday weekends. Be prepared for the occasional summer rain shower in July and August. An umbrella can be a handy tool.

The Sun Valley Golf Course is a meticulously manicured course winding its way through some of the more expensive home sites in the area. The course was redesigned by Robert Trent Jones Jr. This 18-hole course is a great place to rub elbows with the rich and not so famous. Hours are 7am - 7pm with $85 greens fees.

The Elkhorn Golf Course, just on the other side of Dollar Mountain Ski Area from Sun Valley, is another beautiful course. In fact, both Sun Valley and Elkhorn courses are rated top in the state. Elkhorn has elevated tees and sandtraps throughout making it a challenging but fun experience even for the amateur player. This course was also designed by Robert Trent Jones Jr. and has 18-holes. Hours here are 7am - 7pm with $82 greens fees.

The Bigwood Golf Course, designed by Robert Graves, is located 1.5 miles north of Ketchum on Highway 75. Fees are low, the course is great, and the chance of hitting a car with a ball on Highway 75 is better than anywhere else. It is only nine holes but the tees are different for the second round. Hours are from 7am - 8pm and fees are $25 for 9-holes and $38 for 18-holes.

The Warm Springs Golf Course, has 9-holes, and is located against the flanks of Bald Mountain Ski Area up Warm Springs Road in Ketchum. The course is challenging, fun and cost-effective. Be sure to hit the awesome bar and restaurant after a round. Hours are from 7am - 7pm and fees are $19 for 9-holes and $28 for 18-holes.

All the public courses have fully-stocked pro-shops with demos, rentals and carts available. Drinking and driving your golf cart on the city streets is definitely frowned upon by local law enforcement.

Public Golf Courses

Bigwood Golf Course - 105 Clubhouse Dr (208) 726-4024.
Elkhorn Resort Golf Course - Elkhorn Mall (208) 622-3300 / (800) 355-4676.
Sun Valley Resort Golf Course - Sun Valley Road (208) 622-2251 / (800) 786-8259 web: sunvalley.com
Warm Springs Golf Course - 1801 Warm Springs Road (208) 726-3715.

Hiking

You want hiking? We've got hiking, just tell us how far and how strenuous. We have flat, long hikes and short, steep hikes or any combination therein. The locals around Sun Valley are serious trail users, and take great pride in the extensive trail systems we have. These trails are also shared with a great many other users such as equestrians, mountain bikers, trail runners and motorcycles. Be prepared to share the trail with others.

The great thing about hiking around the Sun Valley area is that there are so many places to go, all you need is time. There are tons of mountain lake trails and ridge top trails, all leading to your own little patch of paradise. Almost every hike has water available on it (use a filter or iodine tablets), so be prepared if it is a long one. The mountain lakes are great for swimming, fishing and your canine pals are always welcome.

There are several detailed local hiking guidebooks which are recommended if you decide to do some exploratory hiking in the wilderness areas. They can be purchased at any book or outdoor store.

In early July and August afternoon thunderstorms can come up on you quicker than you think, so be prepared. If you see threatening clouds or are caught in a thunder or lightning storm, be prepared. Lightning lives on the leading edge of storms where they are most violent, and like most annoying things will go away. However, you need to take precaution. Get off any ridges and avoid sitting below trees just to stay dry. Make yourself as small as possible by sitting upright in a fetal position to minimize your contact with the ground. If you aren't sure if there is electricity in the air from an approaching storm, look at the hair on your arms or head to see if it is standing on end. You can also smell ozone in the air when electricity is high. What does ozone smell like? Ever smell a wet dog? Well, there you go. Be prepared for storms by taking an extra warm layer of clothing, some food and water.

The map on the following page shows a "T" which indicates trailhead access to other area trails. Most of the trailheads are quite obvious where they are, but others are a bit hidden. For more detailed explanations, purchase a local hiking guidebook.

Recommendations

1. Adams Gulch Area - Drive 1.5 miles north of Ketchum on Highway 75. Turn left and follow the signs through the houses to the trailhead. There is an overview map of the area in the parking lot. Many hiking options of any length are found in this area.

2. Greenhorn Gulch Area - Drive 6 miles south of Ketchum and turn right onto Greenhorn Gulch Road. Drive another 3.8 miles to the trailhead parking lot. The trailhead is at the west end of the parking area and goes up the hill. Several hiking options in many varying lengths here.

3. Baker Lake - Drive 15.5 miles north of Ketchum on Highway 75 and turn left on Baker Creek Road. Go another 9.4 miles to the end of the road and the parking area/trailhead. From here it is 1.7 miles up a well-maintained trail to the lake.

4. Boulder City - Drive just over 12 miles north of Ketchum on Highway 75 to the top of Phantom Hill and turn right on Boulder Creek Road #158. This can be a rough road, but continue to a fork where the sign points to Boulder Basin. Turn right, cross the creek and continue another 1.5 miles to the registration box and trailhead. From here it is a beautiful 3.5 miles to the old mining town.

5. Bench Lakes - From Stanley, drive 4 miles south on Highway 75 to Redfish Lake Road and turn right. Drive 1.5 miles in, and just <u>after</u> the turn off to the lodge, turn right into the parking lot. The trailhead is at the northwest end of the parking lot. From here it is 3.5 miles to the lakes with scenic vistas the entire way.

6. Bridalveil Falls - From Stanley, drive 5 miles west on Highway 21 and turn left on Stanley Lake Road. After 3.5 miles of washboard road, park in the day-use area by the Inlet Campground. The trailhead is on the south end of the parking area. From here it is 2.3 miles to Lady Face Falls and another 1.3 to Bridalveil Falls. Be careful in early season of the trail being washed over.

Hiking/Outdoor Stores

Backwoods Mountain Sports - Warm Springs Road & Hwy 75 in Ketchum (208) 726-8818.

Elephants Perch - 220 E Sun Valley Rd Ketchum (208) 726-3497.
web: elephantsperch.com, email: perchinfo@svidaho.net

Formula Sports - 460 N Main Ketchum (208) 726-3194.

Riverwear - Hwy 21 in Stanley (208) 774-3592.
web: riverwear.com

Sturtevants - 314 N. Main Ketchum (208) 726-4512.
email: sturtos@micron.net web: sturtos.com

Sturtevants - Hailey (208) 788-7847.

Evening in the Sawtooths - The McBob Collection

53

Hiking Map

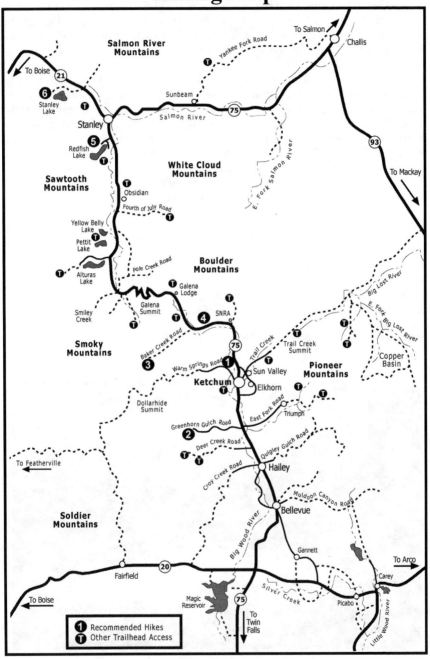

Horseback Riding

Taking a horseback ride while on your visit to Sun Valley is an incredible way to see and experience the natural beauty of the area. Ride to one of the many mountain lakes and imagine the days when cowboys and miners used horses to get to their homes in the mountains.

Many of the local stables offer horse rentals and tours to guide you through our past and present. Local stables and horse outfitters offer one-hour, two-hour, half-day and full-day horse rentals. Some have dinner rides and pack trips or private rides. Most offer some sort of riding instruction as well.

If you don't have much time, then go with one of the Ketchum area stables such as the Sun Valley Horseman's Center who will take you on a tour of the hills around the Sun Valley area. But if you want to get really adventurous and have some extra time, try the Galena Stage Stop or Redfish Lake Corrals for some seriously incredible scenery. Most stables can book you for a ride with one to two day notice, but plan ahead for the busier holiday weekends of the summer.

Horse Outfitters
American Adrenaline Company - Hot Springs Road Challis (208) 879-4700.
Elkhorn Stables - in the Copper Basin at Wildhorse Creek Ranch (208) 726-1865.
Galena Stage Stop - 20 miles N. of Ketchum (208) 726-1735.
Mystic Saddle Ranch - HC 64 Stanley (208) 774-3591.
Pioneer Mountain Outfitters - Stanley (208) 774-3737.
Rawhide Outfitters - Ketchum (208) 756-4276.
Redfish Lake Corrals - Redfish Lake Stanley (208) 774-3311.
Smoky Mountain Outfitters - 317 S River St Hailey (208) 788-9060 / (800) 934-8422.
Sun Valley Horsemen's Center - Sun Valley Road Sun Valley (208) 622-2387.
Super Outfitter Adventures of Sun Valley - 10783 Hwy 75 Bellevue (208) 788-7731. email: jamessuper@sunvalley.net, web: sunvalley-outfitter.com
Valley Ranch Outfitters - Bellevue (208) 774-3470.
Wild Horse Creek Ranch - 20 Miles up Trail Creek Mackay (208) 588-2575.

Hot Springs

This part of Idaho has a wealth of geothermal hot springs. Some are next to the road, while others are a few miles off the beaten path. Aside from a few developed (pay) hot springs, there are far more primitive (non-pay) ones to be enjoyed.

With geothermal hot springs comes a variety of pool temperatures. Some pools have a temperature of 106 degrees on one side and 85 degrees on the other. Some are six inches deep while others are over three feet deep. It all depends on how locals and other tourists have fixed them up after the spring run-off since most all of the hot springs are located next to a stream or river.

Hot springs are fragile areas with unique plant growth near by. Please take extra precaution around these areas. Do not litter or go to the bathroom in the hot springs. Glass containers should be left in the car. Also, being loud and obnoxious is not a nice thing either since most people go to the hot springs for relaxation. Bathing suits or Birthday suits are your choice in the primitive hot springs, while the developed ones require bathing suits. Use your best judgement when children and my parents are present.

Hot Springs - Developed
Easley Hot Springs - 12 miles north of Ketchum on Highway 75 is the outdoor hot springs filled pool with a store and locker room. (208) 726-7522.
Idaho Rocky Mountain Ranch - Highway 75 south of Stanley is a developed private hot spring. (208) 774-3544.

Hot Springs - Primitive
Frenchman's Hot Springs - A favorite spot for locals anytime of the year. The hours are all day until 10pm. Drive about 10 miles up Warm Springs Road and just after crossing the creek on the big metal bridge park on the right. The pools are located next to the creek upstream from the parking area.
Russian John Hot Spring - Located just under 16 miles north of Ketchum on Highway 75 on the left side of the road up on the hillside. The water here is one of the coolest of the hot springs at 94 degrees, but the scenic vistas of the nearby Boulder Mountains are worth the visit.
Salmon River Hot Springs - There are numerous hot springs located along the Salmon River downstream from Stanley, just look for the rising steam. Some are located by Basin Creek and others downstream from there.
Kirkham Hot Springs - About 5 miles east of Lowman and about 50 miles west of Stanley on Highway 21 you'll find Kirkham Campground. At the west end of the campground is the hot springs parking area. Follow the trail down to the falls at the edge of the Payette River.
Bonneville Hot Springs - About 35 miles west of Stanley on Highway 21 is Warm Springs Creek, a campground and the trailhead to Bonneville hot springs and historic bath house. It is a short 15-minute walk through the woods to the springs next to the creek.

Ice-Skating / Ice Shows

Ice-skating in the summer? Here in Sun Valley we have two ice rinks open during the summer, one indoor and one outdoor. Both are located right next to each other outside of the Sun Valley Lodge in the Sun Valley Resort area.

The summer hours for the outdoor skating rink are 10am to 12pm and 1pm to 8pm Sunday through Thursday. Friday and Saturdays the rink is open 10am to 12pm and 1pm to 9pm. The cost is $6.75 for children 12 and under and $7.75 for adults. There is also a $3 ice-skate rental fee on top of admission.

The famous Sun Valley Ice Shows are mid-June through September and start at sundown in the outdoor rink. The ice shows are quite entertaining and feature some of the recent Olympic stars and famous professional skaters, such as Scott Hamilton, Katarina Witt, Oksana Baiul, Elvis Stojko, Kristy Yamaguchi, Viktor Petrenko and Nancy Kerrigan.

Tickets will sell out fast especially on the busy holiday weekends so plan ahead. Treat the family or date-du-jour and go see an ice show. Show tickets are available for the bleachers surrounding the ice rink, but for an extra bonus, the Sun Valley Lodge offers a dinner on their patio along with the ice show. Tickets for the shows are available at the Sun Valley Sports Center (208) 622-2231, located in the Sun Valley Village.

After attending such an awe-inspiring show, you'll want to begin your career as an ice-skater as soon as possible. The Sun Valley ice rink offers skating lessons for either a group or private. Just give the office a call at (208) 622-2194 for more information.

In-line Skating

In-line skating is a great way to spend a few hours exploring the area without getting your feet muddy from the hiking trails or saddle sores from your wild west horseback adventure. Whether you are a beginner or a five-wheeled expert, we promise you some of the best blading you have had all day. The map on the right shows the bike path with a dotted line.

The Bike Path is a paved path, which runs approximately 21 miles from just north of Ketchum all the way down to Bellevue. Its relatively flat surface gently rolls through the Wood River Valley following the old Union Pacific Railroad bed. The trail parallels Highway 75 next to aspen trees, corrals and the Big Wood River. An alternative route would be to follow the bike path around to Sun Valley and up Trail Creek. For some extra excitement, hit the Elkhorn Village loop, the hills are long and steep so be prepared with the proper padding.

A few local sports stores rent in-line skates and protective gear. Don't be too macho and forget the pads, hitting the pavement at 15mph will promise you some of the most ripe and red raspberries you'll ever see.

There are free in-line skating clinics throughout the summer. Check the *Idaho Mountain Express* newspaper for the current dates and times.

In-Line Skating Stores

Formula Sports - 460 N Main Ketchum (208) 726-3194.
Pete Lanes - Sun Valley Road in Sun Valley (208) 622-2276.
Sturtevants - 314 N. Main Ketchum (208) 726-4512.
email: sturtos@micron.net web: sturtos.com
Sturtevants - Hailey (208) 788-7847.

The Bike Path Map

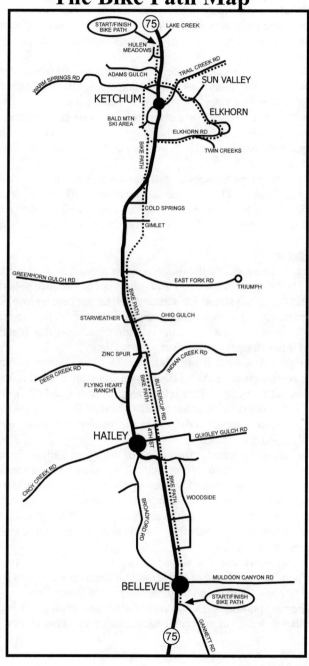

Kayaking/Rafting Whitewater

The Idaho State motto should actually be "The Whitewater State." Sun Valley sits in a great place for access to some of the best whitewater in the United States. People come from all over the world just to get a taste of our world-class western-style whitewater.

Mountain whitewater can be very dangerous if not taken seriously. Early spring run-off from the mountains creates dangerous situations on rivers even for experienced whitewater veterans. If you are going with your own group, take extra precautions for safety. You can never be too safe and besides it's more fun to live and tell about it later. Also, the water here is quite cold and hypothermia can set in quickly. Just be as safe as you can and you'll have the experience of a lifetime.

There are many whitewater-rafting outfitters located around the Sun Valley area and in Stanley. Their businesses are always busy, so book ahead. Some of the outfitters and local stores around Sun Valley and Stanley will rent rafts, kayaks and inflatable kayaks if you want to venture out on your own.

Places To Go

The town of Ketchum sits on the Big Wood River. Just 3 miles north of town on Highway 75 is the Hulen Meadows Pond, which sports two nice holes for kayakers to play in and hone their skills. Lessons are also taught here by local kayak shops. Be sure to park in the gravel parking area provided and not next to the pond. The Big Wood River itself is not a safe and reliable whitewater run due to the amount of trees and other strainers in the river.

As you drive north on Highway 75 over Galena Summit towards whitewater central on the Salmon River, you can stop at another kayaking play wave, known as "Surf City." Turn left on Decker Flats Road #210, cross the river and follow it downstream for about a half-mile until you see the series of waves next to the primitive campground. Park in the meadow and play away. This spot is really only good for kayaks.

Further downstream is the put-in for the Upper Salmon River Run. This is a fun class II/II+ stretch of river which takes you downstream to Stanley. The put-in is about 4.5 miles south of Stanley on Highway 75. There is a pullout next to the bridge, which crosses the Salmon River. Put in on the south side of the bridge and paddle downstream to the obvious paved parking area just before the junction of the highways in Stanley. This is great for inflatable kayaks, smaller rafts and hard-shell kayaks.

Occasionally you see someone floating downstream from Stanley to Sunbeam Dam. This is a nice casual section of the river with great scenery, wonderful fishing opportunities and no whitewater until Basin Creek.

The next popular stretch of river for floaters of all kinds begins at Basin Creek, about 8 miles north of Stanley on Highway 75. This section has two main rapids on it before shooting through Sunbeam Dam. One of the rapids and the bigger of the two is Shotgun Rapids which was featured in an Old Milwaukee Beer commercial many years ago. This section is class III.

The main run on the Salmon River for outfitters and private groups alike is called "The Day Stretch." The put-in is at Sunbeam Dam and continues downstream for about 9 miles to Torrey's. This section has some great surfing on it for kayakers, a canyon section of continuous whitewater and scenery beyond belief. The river parallels the highway making great opportunities for pictures. This section of the river is class III.

There are numerous other whitewater runs around the area. Many of the outfitters listed on this page offer 5-7 day float trips down the Middle Fork and Main Salmon River, as well as 1-day floats down the "Day Stretch." The Payette River drainage begins about 35 miles west of Stanley. If you are venturing into that area on your own, pickup a copy of the whitewater guidebook for Idaho.

Whitewater Shops/Outfitters

Backwoods Mountain Sports - Warm Springs Rd & Hwy 75 Ketchum (208) 726-8818.

Far and Away Adventures - 401 Lewis St Ketchum (208) 726-8888 / (800) 232-8588 email: adventures@far-away.com, web: far-away.com

Mackay Wilderness River Trips - 115 Corrock Ketchum(208) 726-8179 / (800) 635-5336. email: info@mackayriver.com, web: mackay-river.com

Middle Fork River Tours, Inc - 212 Broadford Road Hailey (208) 788-6545 / (800) 445-9738.

Middle Fork Wilderness Outfitter - (208) 726-5999 / (800) 726-0575. email: middlefor@aol.com, web: gorp.com/mfwo

The River Company - Highway 21 Stanley (208) 788-5775. email: 102065.541@compuserve.com

Sawtooth Rentals - Hwy 75 Stanley (208) 774-3409 / (800) 284-3185.

Ski Tek - 191 Sun Valley Rd Ketchum (208) 726-7503. web: ski-tek.com

Sun Valley Rivers Company - (208) 726-7404. web: webcom.com\borchers\sunvly\whitewtr.html

Triangle C/White Water Float - Box 69 Stanley (208) 774-2266 / (800) 303-6258.

Two-M River Outfitters - 30 East Fork Road Ketchum (208) 726-8844.

White Otter Outdoor Adventure - 211 Sun Valley Rd Ketchum (208) 726-4331.

River Rat Express (River Shuttle Service) - Stanley (208) 774-2265.

Whitewater Map

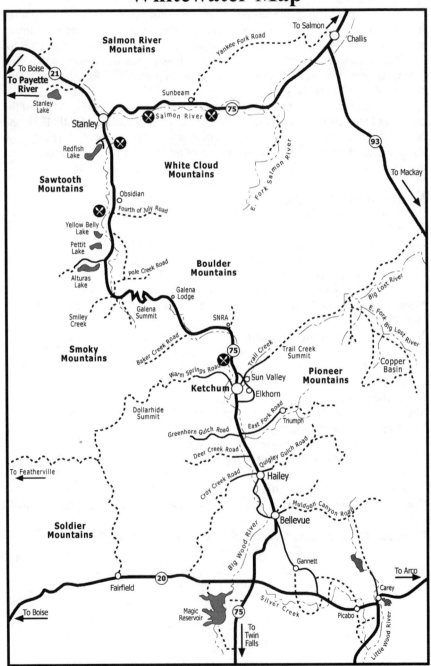

The Middle Fork of the Salmon River - Courtesy Middle Fork River Tours

Music

If music really does make the world go round, then in Sun Valley the world must be flying by. Throughout the summer and fall, the area has a wealth of musical entertainment.

Jazz, soul, pop, reggae, folk and rock groups are constantly flowing through the area performing in some of the local bars, lodges, villages and parks. At anytime of the summer or winter, you'll be able to find some place with your choice of music to enjoy.

Jazz On the Green - Late June through early September at Elkhorn Resort in Sun Valley. Usual start time is 6:30pm, bring your lawn chair and cooler and enjoy the evening listening to some great jazz entertainment. (208) 622-4511.

Concerts at Elkhorn Resort - Concerts are held in the main plaza at Elkhorn throughout the summer. The entire plaza is fenced off and people flood the area for food, drink and music. Groups in the recent past have been Santana, Widespread Panic, Willy Nelson and many more. (208) 622-4511.

Twilight Jazz Series - Starting in July, the River Run Lodge (part of Sun Valley Company) hosts three dates of evening jazz usually starting at 7pm. (208) 726-9491.

Sun Valley Summer Symphony - Attracting large crowds throughout the summer, the symphony plays different pieces with each production. Families can picnic on the grass and enjoy the music beginning at 6:30pm. (208) 622-5607.

Northern Rockies Folk Festival - Around the beginning of August each summer is an entire weekend of folk music in Hailey at Hop Porter Park. Musical guests show up from around the globe. It seems like the whole valley turns out for this one. (208) 788-2700.

Paragliding

Since humans weren't meant to fly, this is as close to heaven as you'll get while you're still alive. And believe me, you'll feel alive when you're soaring 3500 feet above the valley floor enjoying flight in its simplest form.

A paraglide is a parachute-type of "wing" fastened by nylon cords to a harness on you and your pilot/instructor. It packs up small enough to fit in a medium-sized backpack, and with just a few steps off the side of a mountain, you can be airborne.

Sun Valley has one paragliding school for those inclined to learn to do this sport on their own. Because of our natural thermal-quality air, this area allows for a great flying experience.

They have a "no-experience, no-problem" flight for anyone who wants to fly tandem with a professional paragliding pilot for their first and only time. They offer tandem flights off the top of Bald Mountain Ski Area in the winter and summer. The schooling and equipment to do it on your own can cost substantially more. If you are burned out on mountain biking or banging the bumps with your skis, this is a great way to escape for the afternoon in any season.

Paragliding School
Sun Valley Paragliding - 301 Bell Drive #81 Ketchum (208) 726-3332 / (208) 720-0852.

Ridge Soaring - Courtesy of Sun Valley Paragliding

Running/Jogging

Running is such a great form of freedom. The terrain options are endless, and unless you are planning to stay for a year or five, you won't even begin to scratch the surface. We have it all, from a paved bike path (see in-line skating map) to rugged single-track trails of every length and difficulty.

We recommend you purchase the local mountain bike guide, *Good Dirt*, or one of the many local hiking guides for extensive information on trail-running alternatives.

Most of the outdoor shops in town can get you into a good pair of running shoes and any other running paraphenalia you could possibly need. Now put on your shoes and prepare to breathe some fresh mountain air.

Recommendations

1. Wood River Trail System (aka The Bike Path) - This is a paved path which runs approximately 21 miles from just north of Ketchum all the way down to Bellevue. Its relatively flat surface gently rolls through the Wood River Valley following the old Union Pacific Railroad bed. The trail parallels Highway 75 through aspen trees, corrals and along the Big Wood River.

2. Sun Valley Bike Path - This is part of the Sun Valley Trail System, which goes from the east edge of town on Sun Valley Road almost up to Boundary Campground approximately 4.5 miles long.

Trail Running

3. Adams Gulch Area - Drive 1.5 miles north of Ketchum on Highway 75. Turn left and follow the signs through the houses to the trailhead. There is an overview map of the area in the parking lot. Many running options of any length and degree of difficulty.

4. Greenhorn Gulch Area - Drive 6 miles south of Ketchum and turn right onto Greenhorn Gulch Road. Drive another 3.8 miles to the trailhead parking lot. The trailhead is at the west end of the parking area and goes up the hill. Many hiking options in many lengths here.

5. Lake Creek Area - Drive 4 miles north of Ketchum on Highway 75 to the trailhead and parking lot for Lake Creek on the left. The trailhead is at the northern end of the parking lot where there is a map of the trails. This area is not recommended until late spring (mid-June) or early summer (July) due to the seasonal flooding caused by the Big Wood River. There are many trails to choose from.

Skeet Shooting

Skeet shooting is fun for beginners and experts alike. This sport is performed by shooting a shotgun at a moving target made of clay. Since we don't have the typical freeway setting to hone your shooting skills, we offer a couple of gun clubs instead.

The Sun Valley Gun Club (208) 622-2111 is located on Trail Creek Road on the left, just past the lodge and golf course. They are open 10am to 6pm everyday except Monday. Shotguns are available for rent, targets and ammunition is for sale, and private lessons and clinics are by appointment only. Anyone over the age of 11 is welcome to try this sport.

Blaine County Gun Club (208) 788-2681 is located in Ohio Gulch between Hailey and Ketchum off Highway 75. They are open 10am to 3pm Thursdays through Monday. They offer a rifle and piston range, and ammunition is available for sale. They do not offer shotgun rentals or instruction.

Trail Running in Copper Basin - The McBob Collection

Soaring

Have you ever been in a glider? Have you ever flown noiselessly over the mountains riding the thermals? This is what soaring is all about.

After being towed by an airplane to altitude, you are released to glide gracefully around the mountain landscape with a professional pilot as your guide.

Currently there is one company offering year-round soaring in the sun Valley area. The rides start at the Hailey Airport, just off Highway 75, and lasts anywhere from 30-45 minutes. If you've never been on a glider ride, then mark it off your list and go do it. You won't regret it!

Soaring Companies
Sun Valley Soaring - Friedman Airport on Hwy 75 Hailey (208) 788-3054. email: svsoar@aol.com

Soaring the Sun Valley Skyline - Courtesy Sun Valley Soaring

Swimming

If you are in dire need of a swim and there's the ever-so-slight chance that the place you are staying doesn't have a pool, there are some great public facilities to keep you cool.

Blaine County Aquatic Center (208) 788-2144 is located on Fox Acres Road in Hailey. They offer outdoor lap swim in the mornings, host kayak roll classes in the summer and have fun for kids at all times.

Easley Hot Springs (208) 726-7522 is located 15 miles north of Ketchum just off Highway 75. They have a store with locker rooms and showers. The pool is actually a natural hot spring and can vary in temperature from one side of the pool to the other. They are open from the first week of June through October and have amazing views of the Boulder Mountains.

Sun Valley Athletic Club (208) 726-3664 is in downtown Ketchum at 131 First Avenue. They primarily offer indoor lap swimming, but also have a nice workout facility with jacuzzi, steam room and locker rooms. Prices are $15 each for access to the entire club since they don't have a separate pool-only charge.

Hulen Meadows Pond is your au-naturale type of swimming hole. It's actually a pond located on the Big Wood River about 3 miles north of town. Turn left off Highway 75 on Hulen Meadows road and park in the parking area on the right just after the bridge. Be prepared, it's very cold water and you'll be sharing it with kayakers, fishermen and a few dogs.

Tennis

Ever play tennis at high-altitude? If not, get ready to launch your balls out of the court unless you purchase high-altitude tennis balls. This is quite important to keep your sanity and your game in check. You can buy tennis balls at any of the tennis shops in town and at most of the tennis courts with pro-shops.

Our warm spring weather usually has the courts clear of snow by late-April and lasting until late October. It can get a bit breezy in the afternoons on the unprotected courts, but the mountain scenery is so spectacular that you won't even notice. All tennis courts in the area are hard courts.

We have two parks which offer tennis to the public at no charge. They are open all day during daylight hours and are a first-come first-served basis. **Atkinson Park** is located in Ketchum at the north end of Third Avenue next to Hemingway Elementary School. **L. Heagle City Park** is located in Hailey in the Della View subdivision just off War Eagle Drive.

The other tennis courts in the area are also open to the public, but for a charge. They are all very well maintained and are great places to pick up a game if you are alone.

Sun Valley Tennis (208) 622-2156 is located on the east side of the Sun Valley Village next to the parking lot. They have 18 outside courts, a pro-shop and lessons available. They are open seven days a week during summer hours (May-October).

Warm Springs Tennis Club (208) 726-4040 is located off Warm Springs Road in Ketchum. They have 9 outside courts, a pro-shop, lessons, and are open seven days a week during summer hours.

Ironwood Tennis Club (208) 788-9517 is in Hailey in the Woodside Subdivision just off Woodside Boulevard. They have 11 courts, some indoors and some outdoors. This is a great place for getting your tennis-fix in over the winter season.

Alternative Things To Do

Shoshone Ice Caves - Here you can take guided tours of some of Idaho's largest lava ice caves. Spectacular caves in a desert setting. Open from May - Oct. (208) 886-2058. The caves are located on Highway 75 between Shoshone and Bellevue.

Chair Lift Rides - Sun Valley Resort offers rides up the River Run chair lift for $12 per person during summer and winter hours. From the top you can see all of the mountain ranges surrounding Sun Valley. You can eat lunch at the lodge on top, hike to the bottom on a trail, or enjoy the views and ride the lift back down. Call the Sun Valley Sports Center (208) 622-2231 for more information, or simply go to River Run Lodge at the base of Bald Mountain between 10am and 3pm.

Take a Llama To Lunch - This is a great adventure for the entire family to do together. Venture Outdoors, based in Hailey, will pack up the Llama's and take you to a high mountain lake for a terrific time. Guides, leading you and the llama's, will inform you of the areas history and surroundings. (208) 788-5049 / 800-528-LAMA. Email: venout@micron.net, web: ventureoutdoorsidaho.com.

Llama Trek to Norton Lakes - Courtesy Venture Outdoors

Another New Foot and Sunshine - The McBob Collection

The Winter Guide

There are other areas of the world which receive more recognition for their wintertime activities and abundance of snow. Thankfully, the Sun Valley area has remained relatively unknown to the masses. There is no Disneyland, major freeway, or huge population center anywhere close. There is, however, a world-class ski resort, deep powder in the backcountry, about 150km of nordic trails, tons of winter fun for everyone, phenomenal restaurants, and locals without attitudes. This is Sun Valley, Idaho, leave your potato peeler at home and bring your toys, you may never leave.

Activities are listed A - Z

Hockey

Sun Valley is home to the Suns, our local amateur hockey team. They draw in teams from around the country playing games on Friday and Saturday nights. Seeing a hockey game in Sun Valley is a great family activity You can also try out your skating legs at the outdoor rink right next door.

Suns hockey games are a big attraction for locals and tourists alike. The indoor ice rink at Sun Valley can get pretty packed with people cheering them on, especially when the occasional fight erupts. However, the men don't get all the fun, we also are home to the Sunsets, the local amateur womens hockey team. They don't play (or fight) quite as often as the men, but are equally as exciting to watch.

The *Idaho Mountain Express* newspaper comes out on Wednesdays and will have information on any upcoming local Suns hockey games. For more information, call the Suns at (208) 726-6967.

For those of you wanting a quick pick-up hockey game at lunch, the Sun Valley indoor ice rink offers open hockey from 12 Noon - 1:30pm Monday through Friday. The cost is $7 per person. Call the ice rink office for more information at (208) 622-2194.

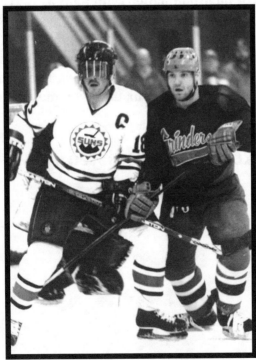

Courtesy Willy Cook / Suns Hockey

74

Ice-Skating

Ice-skating in the winter is a longtime tradition in the area. Many elite skaters use Sun Valley as their training ground due to the year-round rinks at the Lodge. If you don't want to participate yourself, you can enjoy watching them practice from the bleachers next to the outdoor rink or while having lunch at Gretchens in the Sun Valley Lodge.

To supply this great demand for ice-skating, we have two public ice arenas. Sun Valley Resort has an outdoor ice rink catering to the public and guests of the lodge. They are open Mondays, Wednesdays, Thursdays and Sundays from 10am-12pm and 1pm-8pm, Tuesdays 10am-5pm and 6pm-8pm, and on Fridays and Saturdays 10am-12pm and 1pm-9pm. The cost is $6.75 for children 12 and under and $7.75 for adults. There is also a $3 skate rental fee on top of admission. For more information call the ice rink at (208) 622-2194.

The other ice rink is free of charge to the public. It is maintained by the city of Ketchum and located in Atkinson Park, next to Hemingway Elementary School. To get there drive north out of downtown Ketchum onto Warm Springs Road and turn left on 10th Street. You'll see the rink at the end of the road. Skate rentals are available at Sturtevants on Main Street in Ketchum (208) 726-4501 for $5 half day and $10 full day.

Skiing

Downhill Skiing

Skiing at Sun Valley is the main priority of most people visiting and is what made our town famous. And what a great priority! Ketchum has two ski areas, Bald Mountain (the big hill), and Dollar Mountain (the small hill), both owned and operated by The Sun Valley Company. Hailey has one small local ski area out Croy Creek Road to the west of downtown called Rotorun. Fairfield has Soldier Mountain which is about 60 minutes from Hailey on Highway 20 towards Boise.

Bald Mountain has 13 lifts and 64 runs, seven high-speed quads, four triples and two doubles. The vertical drop is 3,250 feet and the summit has an altitude of 9,150 feet. It has 2054 skiable acres, and snowmaking covers 603 acres. The longest run is three miles long and with the thirteen lifts they can move 23,380 people per hour up the mountain. Basically, what these stats tell you is that if you want to make your legs burn, and burn they will, this is your mountain. There are beginner slopes off the top of the mountain, plenty of tree skiing and virtually no lift-lines. The season runs from Thanksgiving to the middle of April.

Lift tickets are $54 full-day adult and $30 full-day child. Half-day afternoon-only rates are slightly less. They offer 2- through 7-day tickets without much of a discount, but do give seniors (65 and older) tickets for $36 full-day.

Sun Valley Resort also offers ski and snowboard lessons for all ages. Lessons are taught at both Bald Mountain and Dollar Mountain. For more information, call the Sun Valley Ski and Snowboard School for clinics, group or private lessons (208) 622-2248.

The thing to remember about Sun Valley Resort is that they don't give much of anything away. The food is expensive everywhere on the mountain, however, the Seattle Ridge Lodge has some of the best. The lift tickets are expensive, but in return you get some of the best skiing in North America. The magazines and reader polls have consistently put Sun Valley at the top. If you ask any of the locals, they'll agree and that's why they are here.

Dollar Mountain has 4 double lifts, and 13 runs. The vertical drop is 1,526 feet and the summit has an altitude of 6,638 feet. They have snow making all over the mountain and the lifts can move 4,800 people per hour. Dollar Mountain is known as the beginner mountain with mostly gentle slopes throughout. Its close proximity to the Sun Valley Village makes it a great kids ski area while the grown-ups hit the bigger Bald Mountain.

Lift tickets are $25 full-day adult and $17 full-day child. Half-day afternoon-only rates are slightly less. New for the 1998-1999 season is a serious snowboard half-pipe on the west end of the ski area.

For any information on the Sun Valley ski areas, call the Sun Valley Sports Center at (208) 622-2231or call the Sun Valley Ski Report at (800) 635-4150.

Downhill Skiing Rental/Sales/Service
Downhill Service - 1007 B Warm Springs Road Ketchum (208) 726-1825.
Formula Sports - 460 N Main Ketchum (208) 726-3194.
Paul Kenney's - Base of Warm Springs Ketchum (208) 726-7474.
web: pkski.com
Pete Lanes - Sun Valley Village Sun Valley (208) 622-2276.
Pete Lanes - Base of Warm Springs Ketchum (208) 622-6354.
Pete Lanes - Base of River Run Ketchum (208) 622-6123.
Ski-Tek - 191 Sun Valley Rd Ketchum (208) 726-7503. web: ski-tek.com
Sturtevants - 314 N. Main Ketchum (208) 726-4512.
Email: sturtos@micron.net   Web: http://www.sturtos.com
Sturtevants - Base of Warm Springs Ketchum (208) 726-SKIS.
Sturtevants - Main St & Carbonate Hailey (208) 788-7847.
Sun Summit Ski & Cycle - 791 Warm Springs Rd Ketchum (208) 726-0707.
Sun Summit South - 507 S Main Hailey (208) 788-6006.
Sun Valley Outfitters - Elkhorn Resort Plaza Sun Valley (208) 622-3400.
The Waxroom - 131 2nd St Ketchum (208) 726-7595.

Heli-Skiing the Sun Valley Backcountry - Courtesy Sun Valley Heli-Guides

Backcountry Skiing & Touring

The mountains around the Sun Valley area offer all kinds of backcountry experiences for the novice and expert alike. Whether you want to take a relatively easy tour to one of the mountain lakes or want to put some serious turns down on some wilderness slopes, we have it all.

For easier touring, follow any of the canyons north of town. They are flat to moderate tours with the possibility of making turns on some open slopes fairly close by. For the more serious backcountry skiing experience, drive anywhere north of Ketchum, eye your slope, put on your skins and give it a go. Most people head up to Galena Summit about 25 miles north of Ketchum due to its close proximity to the highway and gentle open slopes.

Safety is a key ingredient to any backcountry experience, whether you are out for a casual tour or looking for the steeps. Always go with a partner, leave a note in your car where you are going and when you plan on returning, carry extra clothes, food and water, a shovel and transceiver for everyone in your party. There is NO excuse for skimping on safety. If in doubt, don't go. Call the Avalanche Center Hotline at (208) 788-1200 x.8027 for details on avalanche danger for the day. If you see any avalanche release, please call the Avalanche Center Observer Hotline at (208) 788-1200 x.8028 to let them know where and what you saw. Any and all avalanche information is helpful, along with your joke of the day. You can also find them on the internet at www.avalanche.org.

Backcountry Skiing Rental/Sales/Service

Backwoods Moutain Sports - Warm Springs Road & Hwy 75 in Ketchum (208) 726-8818.
Elephants Perch - 220 E Sun Valley Rd Ketchum (208) 726-3497.
email: perchinfo@svidaho.net, web: elephantsperch.com
Sturtevants - 314 N. Main Ketchum (208) 726-4512.
email: sturtos@micron.net, web: sturtos.com

Important Phone Numbers

Sun Valley Avalanche Center Hotline (208) 788-1200 x.8027.
Sun Valley Avalanche Center Observer Hotline (208) 788-1200 x.8028.
web: avalanche.org

Heli-Skiing

Being guided into the backcountry via a helicopter is one thing that everyone should experience before they go to the great ski area in the sky. The thrill of being wisped away to an untracked high mountain slope is incredible and one that I highly recommend. Our local guide service does a wonderful job finding you piles of the white stuff and all in a very safe manner. They tend to get booked up pretty quickly over the busy holiday weekends, so plan ahead and take the day-trip of a lifetime, you won't regret it.

Sun Valley Heli-Guides run their operation at 260 1st Ave N. in Ketchum. A typical full-day of heli-skiing costs $500 and half-days $300. They offer group discounts with low season rates starting in January. For more information call (208) 622-3108, or email: svheli@sunvalley.net, or web: svheli-ski.com.

Cross-Country Skiing

The Wood River Valley has become known as the Mecca for cross-country skiers. We have over 150 km of groomed trails, more than almost any area in North America. Most of the trails are maintained by the county and groomed by rather sophisticated machinery. This means there is a small charge for trail day use, with season passes available. Other trails are managed and maintained by Sun Valley Resort, which has their own nordic center. All of the trails in the area are groomed for classic and skate skiing.

Rental equipment is available for nordic skiing from Backwoods Mountain Sports, The Elephants Perch in Ketchum, Sturtevants, the Sun Valley Nordic Center and at Galena Lodge. On busy weekends, plan ahead and get your equipment early, it goes fast.

The North Valley Trails

This area is comprised of Lake Creek, which is 4 miles north of Ketchum; North Fork, 8 miles north of Ketchum; Murphy's Bridge, 10.5 miles north of Ketchum; Billy's Bridge, 18 miles north of Ketchum; Prairie Creek, 18.5 miles north of Ketchum; Galena Lodge Trails, 24 miles north of Ketchum; and The Boulder Mountain Trail, which goes from the SNRA to Galena Lodge. For grooming and trail information call (208) 726-6662. Daily fees are $7 per person, with passes available at all outdoor shops in the area.

The Boulder Mountain Trail

This is a 30km groomed trail, which goes from the Sawtooth National Recreation (SNRA) Headquarters, 8 miles north of Ketchum, all the way up to Galena Lodge, 24 miles north of Ketchum.

As you drive on Highway 75 between the nordic trail areas, you will notice access points to the Boulder Mountain Trail off to the side. Many people just park in the small pullouts and ski out and back on the trail. The only portion of the trail where dogs are allowed is from Easley Hot Springs to the SNRA.

Each February, close to one-thousand nordic skiers brave the temperatures and ski in the Boulder Mountain Tour, a race from Galena Lodge to the end of the trail at the SNRA. It is part of a national nordic race series attracting top competitors from around the country.

Lake Creek is located 4 miles north of Ketchum on the left side of Highway 75. The skiing area is against the foothills on the west-side of the Big Wood River. This nordic ski area has 15.5km of groomed trails. It is a training ground for local nordic teams and has some great hills to get your heart pumping. No dogs are allowed here.

North Fork Trail is located 8 miles north of Ketchum on Highway 75. Park at the SNRA headquarters on the right, and the trail begins on the north side of the parking area. The 4km groomed trail is relatively flat and can get a bit windy in the afternoons and evenings. Dogs are welcome on the North Fork Trail.

Billy's Bridge is located 18 miles north of Ketchum on Highway 75 on the right side of the road in a big pullout. It has a slightly hilly 8km figure-eight groomed trail which winds around the foothills of the Boulder Mountains. Dogs are welcome here.

Prairie Creek is located 18.5 miles north of Ketchum on Highway 75 on the left side of the road in the parking (pullout) area. This trail system has 7.5km of groomed trails but also has access to the Boulder Mountain Trail. This is one of the prettiest trails around due to the seclusion in the high alpine canyon. No dogs are allowed here.

Galena Lodge is located 24 miles north of Ketchum on Highway 75. You'll know you're there when you see the rustic cabin and parking area on the right side of the road. This lodge is one of the most amazing places for beauty and sports. It is owned by the community and has over 50km of groomed trails. They offer lessons, have rentals and a restaurant with incredible food. You don't have to be a skier to enjoy this place, just sitting, relaxing and warming your toes is enough for many people. There are approximately 9km of dog trails available.

Sun Valley Nordic Center
If you enjoy skiing corduroy, then this is your kind of place. Director Hans Muehlegger makes sure that all 40km of their trails are groomed perfectly each day. There are hills, flats, wildlife, streams and the views are incredible. They offer beginner to expert instruction, lunch tours, and a great pro-shop.

The Wood River Trail
If you like to ski long and straight with not much elevation gain or loss, then try out the Wood River Trail for your nordic pleasures. In the summer this is known as "the Bike Path," but when winter rolls around you can ski from north of Ketchum all the way to Bellevue. In early spring an event called "Ski The Rails" goes from Ketchum to Hailey. You can access the Wood River Trail from virtually any spot along Highway 75, just look for the skiers and the dogs. For a detailed map, see page 59.

Cross-Country Skiing Rental/Sales/Service
Backwoods Moutain Sports - Warm Springs Road & Hwy 75 in Ketchum (208) 726-8818.
Elephants Perch - 220 E Sun Valley Rd Ketchum (208) 726-3497.
email: perchinfo@svidaho.net, web: elephantsperch.com
Galena Lodge - 24 miles north of Ketchum on Highway 75 (208) 726-4010.
Sturtevants of Hailey - Main St & Carbonate in Hailey (208) 788-7847.
email: sturtos@micron.net, web: sturtos.com
Sun Valley Nordic Center - Sun Valley Road Sun Valley (208) 622-2251.
web: sunvalley.com

Important Phone Numbers
North Valley & Wood River Valley Trails Grooming Hotline (208) 726-6662.

Cross-Country Skiing Map

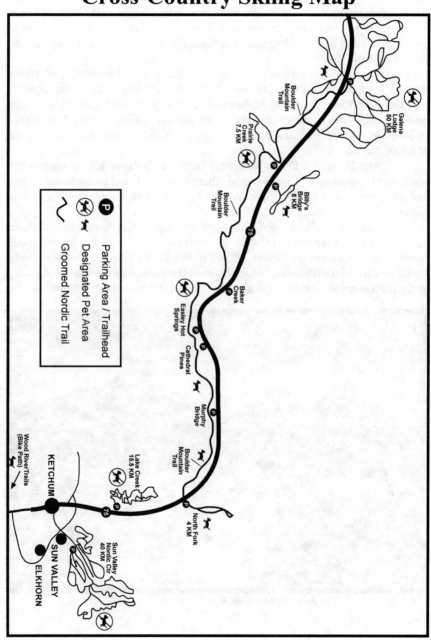

Parking Area / Trailhead

Designated Pet Area

Groomed Nordic Trail

Galena Lodge 50 KM

Boulder Mountain Trail

Prairie Creek 7.5 KM

Billy's Bridge 8 KM

Boulder Mountain Trail

Baker Creek

Easley Hot Springs

Cathedral Pines

Murphy Bridge

Boulder Mountain Trail

Lake Creek 15.5 KM

North Fork 4 KM

Wood River Trails (Bike Path)

KETCHUM

SUN VALLEY

ELKHORN

Sun Valley Nordic Ctr 40 KM

Sledding

It's just like being a kid again. We think this should be the next Olympic event, especially if you've done your training in Sun Valley. Unfortunately there are no places in town to rent sledding gear, but make the small investment, buy a plastic sled and hit the slopes!

There are quite a few places to go sledding in and around the Ketchum area. The most popular is the obvious hill next to the stop light at the corner of Sun Valley and Saddle Roads. At the main street stop light in Ketchum, drive east on Sun Valley Road until you see the hill on the left in about a mile. Parking is a major problem here, so please don't park in any driveways or on Sun Valley Road blocking traffic.

Another spot is Dollar Mountain Ski Area. You can hike as high as you want, just be cautious of lift tower and other sledders. The ski area closes at 4pm and takes until about 4:30pm for the crowds to clear. Watch out for the big grooming machines in the early evenings here.

There are pullouts along Highway 75 north of Ketchum where sledders can enjoy a brisk hike and fun slides close enough to the road for mom and dad to watch from the warmth of the car. Please remember that as innocent as sledding looks, be careful for obstacles hidden beneath the surface of the snow and to stay away from steep slopes due to avalanche danger. Be safe and have fun!

The Beautiful Sawtooth Mountains - The McBob Collection

Sleigh Rides

An evening ride in a horse-drawn sleigh can be the ultimate topper on any Sun Valley vacation. Imagine the romance of floating through the snow with only the sounds of bells around a horse's neck . . . it'll carry you away.

But don't feel you have to get out in the hills for a sleigh ride, you can take part in this fun right in downtown Ketchum. Kesha's Carriage Co offers rides on a wheeled carriage throughout town; A Winter's Feast offers sleigh rides in conjunction with dinner at yurts at the Warm Springs Ranch just two minutes from downtown; Warm Springs Sleighs offer rides on the hour at the Warm Springs Ranch; Sun Valley Company offers sleigh rides in conjunction with dinner at Trail Creek Cabin. All sleigh rides are a winter-only activity with the exception of Kesha's which runs throughout the year.

Take advantage of the beautiful scenery and romantic settings on a sleigh ride in Sun Valley. Most companies will allow private rentals for special occasions.

Sleigh/Carriage Companies
Warm Springs Sleighs - (208) 726-3322.
A Winter's Feast - Warm Springs Ranch in Ketchum (208) 788-7665.
Kesha's Carriage Co - (208) 788-9405.
Super Outfitter Adventures of Sun Valley - 10783 Hwy 75 Bellevue (208) 788-7731. email: jamessuper@sunvalley.net, web: sunvalleyoutfitter.com
Sun Valley Resort - Sun Valley Road Sun Valley (208) 622-2135 / (800) 786-8259, web: sunvalley.com
Wild Horse Creek Ranch - 20 Miles up Trail Creek Mackay (208) 588-2575.

Courtesy Kesha's Carriage Company

Snowboarding

Sun Valley is a snowboarding paradise. Both Bald and Dollar Mountains have unlimited access to snowboarders, although during the busy holiday season two runs on Seattle Ridge on Bald Mountain become closed only to snowboarders. A small price to pay.

Dollar Mountain is now home to a professional half-pipe on the lower west end of the area. This is a new attraction for the 1998-99 season, so after-hour rules are not set in stone, but please respect any closure signs.

The backcountry north of Ketchum is another popular place for snowboarding. Near Galena Summit on Highway 75, there are many slopes to choose from with car shuttles possible and rock jumps plentiful. If you plan on going into the backcountry, please have safety equipment and avalanche knowledge. Riding in the backcountry is fun, but not worth dying for. Be safe, have fun and leave the attitude at home.

Snowboard Rental/Sales/Service

The Board Bin - 180 4th St Ketchum (208) 726-1222.
email: boardbin@micron.net, web: boardbin.com
Paul Kenny's Ski & Sports - Base of Warm Springs Ketchum (208) 726-7474.
web: pkski.com
Sturtos - 314 N. Main St. Ketchum (208) 726-4512.
email: sturtos@micron.net, web: sturtos.com
Sturtevants - Main St & Carbonate Hailey (208) 788-7847.
Sturtevants - Base of Warm Springs Ketchum (208) 726-SKIS.
Sun Summit South - 507 S Main Hailey (208) 788-6006.

Important Phone Numbers

Sun Valley Avalanche Center Hotline (208) 788-1200 x.8027.
Sun Valley Avalanche Center Observer Hotline (208) 788-1200 x.8028.
web: avalanche.org

Backcountry Boardin' - The McBob Collection

Snowmobiling

So you want to go screaming through the powder in a gorgeous setting at the base of the Boulder or Sawtooth Mountains? Welcome home. Actually the Wood River and Sawtooth Valleys are home to a wide variety of wintertime sports, but according to some destination snowmobile magazines, we have some of the best snowmobiling anywhere!

Don't let your excitement get in the way of safety. Please be prepared for the backcountry. Avalanches do happen, so plan ahead and know your limits. Avalanche transceivers and shovels are a must! Know how to use them and read signs of avalanche activity. Snowmobilers are killed every year in the area due to getting swallowed up by a slide because they were somewhere they shouldn't have been. High-marking is the main cause of snowmobiler avalanche deaths. Call the Avalanche Hotline for a daily forecast and information (208) 788-1200 x.8027.

Please watch for wildlife and do not chase them. Animals having to live through the winters have a very conservative fat reserve they need to survive on. When they are chased, their reserve is consumed and they lose their fat and can starve to death. How would you like an elk on a snowmobile to chase you while you try to run through 10 feet of snow? There is strict enforcement to ride in snowmobile permitted areas only and hefty fines for harassing wildlife.

Baker Creek is 15.5 miles north of Ketchum on Highway 75. The parking area is next to the highway with trails leading every which way. This is one of the most popular areas to start from and can get rather crowded. There is a nordic trail which passes through here on the south side of the highway, please go slow and watch for the "skinny skiers", they're not worth many points anyway.

Smiley Creek is 37.5 miles north of Ketchum on Highway 75. There is a nice lodge here with a restaurant, snowmobile rentals and knowledge of local trails, even though you can pretty much go anywhere.

Stanley is now considered the snowmobile capital of the world, due to the remarkable terrain and groomed trails. Stanley is approximately 58 miles north of Ketchum at the junction of Highways 75 and 21. There are snowmobile rentals in town, food, gas and whatever else you could possibly want.

Rental
Mulligan's Sun Valley Adventures - PO Box 381 Sun Valley (208) 726-9137.
Sawtooth Rentals - Hwy 75 Stanley (208) 774-3409 / (800) 284-3185.
Smiley Creek Lodge - 37.5 miles north of Ketchum (208) 774-3547.

Sales/Service
Pro-Line Sport - 345 Lewis St Ketchum (208) 726-4221.
Woodside RV Center - 4040 Glenbrook Dr Hailey (208) 788-4005.
Williams Motorsports - 1215 S. Main Bellevue (208) 788-7577.

Snowshoeing

Snowshoeing is one of the oldest forms of transportation around, only now we consider it a sport. "Oh great," you're thinking, "all I need is more gear." Well, right you are, only you don't have to buy snowshoes when there are plenty of places to rent them right here in town.

What does it take to snowshoe? First it takes a bit of snow, once you have that and are dressed for the cold, all you need to do is find the proper equipment and walk normally. Snowshoeing is the only sport where you are qualified to do it from the ages of 2 to 100. If you can walk, you can snowshoe.

There are a number of snowshoe specific locations. However, don't feel limited to going just to these areas. Feel free to explore on your own and make a trail where you want. If you do venture out on your own, be sure you know how to travel in the backcountry. Carry proper safety equipment such as avalanche transceivers, a shovel (one per person), and extra clothing, food and water. You never know what can happen in the middle of winter in Idaho's mountains. If traveling on your own doesn't thrill you, check out any of the posted snowshoe trails around the valley, they are safe and volunteers maintain them on a regular basis.

Most snowshoe areas are close to the nordic skiing trails. Snowshoe-specific trails are located at North Fork, Sun Valley Nordic Center, Prairie Creek, Billy's Bridge and Galena Lodge. Please do not walk on the nordic trails since the cleats on the snowshoes can damage the trail. Refer to the nordic skiing map on page 81 for locations of the trails listed above.

Rental/Sales/Service

Backwoods Moutain Sports - Warm Springs Road & Hwy 75 in Ketchum (208) 726-8818.
Elephants Perch - 220 E Sun Valley Rd Ketchum (208) 726-3497.
web: elephantsperch.com, email: perchinfo@svidaho.net
Galena Lodge - 24 miles north of Ketchum on Highway 75 (208) 726-4010.
Sturtevants - 314 N. Main Ketchum (208) 726-4512.
email: sturtos@micron.net, web: sturtos.com
Sun Valley Nordic Center - Sun Valley Road Sun Valley (208) 622-2251.
web: sunvalley.com

Galena Lodge - The McBob Collection

Yurts

Yurts are canvas-walled tents located in our backcountry areas. They are typically octagonal-shaped and can sleep anywhere from 8 - 15 people. Yurts contain all the basic necessities of home, such as a kitchen, pans, bunks with pads, fuel, wood and wood burning stoves. Some yurts even have a wood burning hot tub or sauna, a definite plus on the luxury scale.

People use the yurts in the winter season for a place to go backcountry skiing. They are mostly located in areas where great skiing is close by, but don't let the lure of untracked powder get the best of you. If you are backcountry skiing or snowboarding into a yurt, know how to travel safely through avalanche prone terrain.

Each company renting yurts offers the use of a backcountry guide to orient you with the yurt basics and will show you to some of the better slopes. This is highly recommended especially if you don't know what you're doing. Each company will also provide a guide just to lead you in if you have never been to that particular yurt, regardless of your backcountry experience, knowledge and ability. They will also give you a list of equipment you will need, liability forms, right of first born, etc.

If you need someone to ski part of your yurt supplies into the yurt to avoid carrying a 50-pound pack, call Backcountry Express listed below. For a fee, they'll carry all your gear. After loading your pack and feeling how heavy it is, you may want to reconsider. Also, if you are in need of backcountry rental gear, check the listing under "Backcountry Skiing" for rental locations.

Avalanche courses are available through the Sun Valley Avalanche Center and Sawtooth Mountain Guides. They are well worth any expense to become more knowledgable in the backcountry.

The map on the following page shows the location of yurts available to rent. The three yurts by Redfish Lake are run by Sawtooth Mountain Guides, while Galena Lodge runs their own yurt. The three yurts around Baker Creek are run by Sun Valley Trekking, and the yurt in the Pioneer Mountains is run by Sun Valley Heli-Guides.

Yurt Rental Companies
Galena Lodge - Highway 75, 20 miles N of Ketchum (208) 726-4010.
Sawtooth Mountain Guides - P.O. Box 18 Stanley (208) 774-3324.
email: getaway@sawtoothguides.com, web: sawtoothguides.com
Sun Valley Trekking - PO Box 2200 Sun Valley (208) 726-1002.
Sun Valley Heli-Guides - 260 1st Ave. N Ketchum (208) 622-3108.
email: svheli@sunvalley.net, web: svheli-ski.com.
Backcountry Express - PO Box 6046 Ketchum (208) 788-1917.

Yurt Map

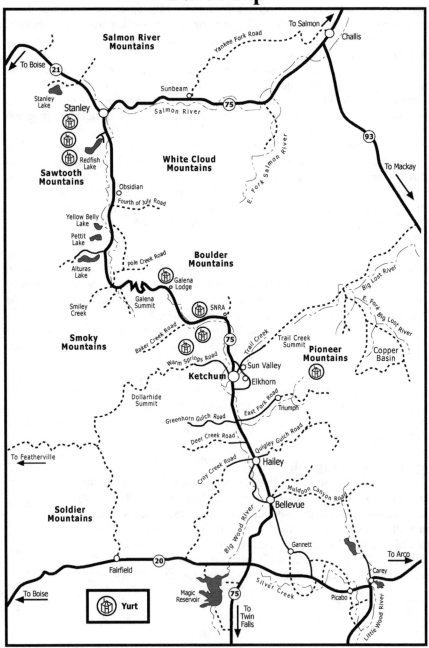

Hiking to Williams Peak Yurt - The McBob Collection

About the Authors

Darla and Greg McRoberts have lived in the Sun Valley, Idaho area for over twelve years. Both Idaho natives, they met in Sun Valley and eventually married here where they still reside today. Greg works full-time as sales reps in the outdoor industry, and when Darla can pull herself off the local trails, she spends her time working on various design and art projects. Together, they write regional and national guidebooks for the activities they love.

When they are not at home, you can find them either trail running, mountain biking, rock climbing, backpacking or backcountry skiing somewhere in the world.

Springtime "research" down south

Notes

Notes

Notes

Notes

Notes

Notes